The Marriage Option

the

marriage

option

by David Sammons

Beacon Press   Boston

*To Rosemary, with whom
I began the journey of
marriage, and to Janis,
whom I love and with
whom I intend to soar
until the end*

Copyright © 1977 by David Sammons

Beacon Press books are published under the auspices
of the Unitarian Universalist Association

Published simultaneously in Canada by
Fitzhenry & Whiteside Limited, Toronto

Printed in the United States of America

(Hardcover) 9 8 7 6 5 4 3 2 1

Library of Congress Cataloging in Publication Data

Sammons, David.
   The marriage option.
   Bibliography: p.
   1. Marriage—United States. 2. Family—United
States. 3. Divorce—United States. 4. Interpersonal
relations. I. Title.
HQ536.S33   301.42'0973   76–48531
ISBN 0–8070–2746–4

Contents

Introduction

Why write a book? That's a question I have asked myself lots of times, feeling that inside me there was one, especially one about relationships. This thought was stronger than ever when I was asked to think about a book on weddings, a "cookbook" sort of text on how to do your own. Having worked with several hundred couples who have wanted to write their own ceremonies, I am thoroughly committed to the idea that this is the only good way for a couple to announce and affirm their marriage, at least from the standpoint of the humanistic religious tradition in which I stand. But there are several wedding cookbooks already on the market, including an evolving mimeographed collection of my own. Another is not needed.

Then I had the chance to attend a series of seminars featuring Dr. Margaret Mead, held annually for members of the therapeutic community by the Department of Psychiatry at the University of Cincinnati's College of Medicine. No matter what subject she addresses, Dr. Mead is always stimulating, and her subjects this time centered around character development, crisis intervention, and marriage. I was particularly impressed by her interaction with panelists who at her request had read a book called *Seven Perfect Marriages That Failed*. Responding to them, she gave her reasons for believing that marriage as an institution is not about to disappear as a preferred sort of relationship between committed adults, though it is undergoing profound changes and is under great stress. There are too many positive reasons for it to exist, she claimed, for it to be replaceable. What she said set my mind in motion, and out of the process came the idea for this book.

Over the years I have thought a lot about marriage, both its hopes and its problems. A few of my thoughts have found their way into print—some articles written for journals, such as *The Single Parent*, a publication of Parents Without Partners, whose local chapter I served as an adviser for several years. Some have appeared in the local press. Most have been presented as sermons, later to be distributed through the favorite medium of a minister, mimeographed copies. The response to my ideas was usually good, but at the time it seemed enough to cast my thoughts to the winds, as it were, and let it go at that.

What Dr. Mead said helped coalesce my thinking. I realized that there was a strand about human relationships that ran not only through these articles and sermons but through my own life as well. It was a valuing of close, intimate—what I would call "centered"—relationships, in which people come to know each other in a depth of sharing not found in the ordinary relationship. For me, this sort of relationship and the discovery of its existence is what gives both the content to a marriage and the reason for its being. This is as much a personal as a theoretical statement. Not only has my discovery of such a relationship created the feeling in my life that it was time to celebrate and affirm it in a wedding, but the discovery of its demise also has led to a decision to end a marriage. Fortunately, at least from my perspective, I am "twice born." I have married again and share in a beautiful and fulfilling marital relationship with a woman whom I intend to love and respect for a long time. I hope, for a lifetime.

What follows in this book is an odyssey through the meanings and realities of the marriage option, informed by both professional observation and personal experience. You will find me here and many of the people with whom I have been involved. I know of no other way to approach such a personal subject, and it is my hope that in revealing myself you will be prompted to look more closely at yourself. For this reason you will find a lot of "I's" and "we's" in the chapters ahead. I will be trying to engage you in a mental dialogue in which you will need to think about your own attitudes and feelings about marriage.

This book has at least three purposes: The first is to be a book that would be useful for a couple to read when they are thinking about formalizing their relationship by being wed. It will raise the question: why be married? The second is to be a book that married partners will find useful as their marriage evolves, changes, and encounters either problems or new possibilities. In serving this function it is not meant to be a marriage manual, but more a collection of reflections—a provoker of thought and care-fullness. Finally, this is a book about human relationships, *per se*. Much of what needs to be said about the special centered relationship celebrated in marriage also needs to be said about other sorts of relationships. The same is true in reverse. For this reason it is important to talk about friendship, for instance, without which no marriage can succeed.

These three purposes prompt me to discuss some things one might not expect to find in a book about the marriage option—such as divorce. It is my contention that a primary quality of any serious relationship is the quality of "knowing." The knowing of the people involved in a decision to marry ought to be one of knowing that the marriage is intended to last. But also included should be an awareness that the two have personal resources available and the commitment of concern required for the ending of the marriage—if it should become necessary.

An image I often use to symbolize the beginning of marriage is jumping off a cliff. But the jump does not entail a plunge to the rocks below. It entails hang gliding—soaring with one's partner in a beautiful and satisfying flight. Only a careless person would take such a leap without a parachute, however. What the parachute represents is knowledge about what to do and the courage and strength to do it, if the flight fails.

Most of what I have to say is on the positive side of marriage, however. I view marriage as the most deep and satisfying of all human relationships. The marriage option has stood the test, as Dr. Mead suggests, and remains a good and viable option for the many people who choose it.

Creating this book has been an exciting adventure for me—part of a process of considering the important issues of life and of human relationships that I intend to continue for the rest of my days. What follows has informed me as I have moved into and out of, then back into, the centered relationship of marriage. My hope is that it will be both informative and an adventure for you.

1

Trying Out the Options

On one of those dark and foggy nights common to the San Francisco area a car full of theologs crossed the bridge at the lower end of the Bay and crept up a winding road toward La Honda. A group of about-to-be-ministers was on its way to the hideout of Ken Kesey and an encounter with the "Merry Pranksters," who were soon to become central figures in the rising counterculture of the late 60s. It was an exciting, eye-opening night of initiation into a whole new world for most of us.

A lot has happened since that night in the fall of 1964. Most of the students from Starr King School for the Ministry who had made the trip to Kesey's are settled in churches and have lifestyles much more ordinary than they might have fantasized while with the Pranksters. Not that many of us haven't tried to be pioneers in our personal and professional lives. It's just that what seemed so hip in the 60s lost its allure in the face of the ongoing realities of life.

During the 60s and early 70s many people, from "flower children" dropping out of society to ministers trying to stay creatively in it, became intrigued with the idea of living out new options to conventional lifestyles. This included everything from using drugs, to challenging institutional forms, to seeking to humanize work, to adopting new patterns of relationships. All of this behavior sent shockwaves through the culture, and for a while, particularly during the period after the ghetto rebellions and during the agonizing over our country's involvement in the war in Southeast Asia, it seemed as though everything was up for grabs.

The end of World War II had brought with it a freeing up of society. In spite of the blight of McCarthyism and the continued oppression of large minority segments of our population, the years following Hiroshima were flush ones. With big-bumper cars and a flood of new products, we came to think of ourselves as an "affluent society." People became more mobile and wealthy, and their lifestyles began to reflect it. While the Pranksters in La Honda may have seemed like revolutionaries to most, they were really no more than products of a society changing more rapidly than it realized.

With the assassination of President Kennedy, the riots in our cities, the growing morass of the Vietnam War, and the explosion of the counterculture into public consciousness, the change could no longer be denied. For some it was a dreadful shock. For others it seemed a permit to take leaps into the future. This phenomenon can be most dramatically seen in what has happened to relational styles during the past decade.

When I was a youngster looking ahead and thinking about what my life would be like, I thought it would closely follow that of my fathers and brothers: I would work hard to become good at sports, stay popular during adolescence, find a sweetheart and get married, and then live happily ever after with my wife and four children. I tried hard to make that vision come true. It didn't work out quite as I had planned, even though I did manage to try out all of the things I've mentioned—including, in a flush of pre-Pill exuberance, the fathering of four children.

By the mid-60s this vision was changing as I began to encounter a proliferation of new models of lifestyles. The same was happening to many others. All a person needed to convince him or her of how varied were the lifestyle possibilities was to look at the "Personals" in the *Los Angeles Free Press* or any of the other underground papers popular at the time.

For all its confusion, this opening up of personal options was healthy. American society had become too depersonalized. As its institutions had made more and more demands, people drew in on themselves. The 50s and early 60s were not only years of growing affluence, they were also years typified by "organization men" and neurotic housewives; the man in the gray flannel suit and "Suzy Homemaker" were no joke. Many Americans needed and wanted to break out of the constraints they felt had been placed on their personal and professional lives.

All sorts of therapies, group processes, and experimental styles of living arose in response to these needs and desires, and they grew increasingly popular as it became clear that social activism was doing little to bring about greater social justice or an end to the war in Southeast Asia. Because of this there was a turning inward among the more liberal and adventurous Americans, and a centering on relationships as they did so. This meant experimenting with communes, group marriage, swinging and swapping, the coming into the open of the gay and bisexual scenes, an "epidemic" of divorce (which continues unabated), and the resurgence of single adulthood as an acceptable alternative to marriage. Many began to believe that marriage, as an institution, had outlived its usefulness and ought to be replaced with other forms of relationships.

THE COMMUNAL MOVEMENT

The most attention-getting of the new forms tried was the group-living experience of the commune. Many of us who were attracted to such experiments wanted not only to broaden our sensitivity and awareness of other people, but to change our lives. We wanted to live apart with a group of like-minded individuals and create a new way of life, building our own miniculture from scratch. We believed that we could create the kind of environment in which it would be possible to experience life with an authenticity and honesty impossible in the larger society. Like earlier utopians, we thought we would be able to create an ideal life by communing together.

There was a lot of naïveté in the communal movement, however. Creating and maintaining an ideal society proved to be a more difficult task than most of us could manage. Few communes provided enough structure, enough privacy, enough group process, enough leadership, even enough reason-to-be, to survive. Most of us who tried to live communally discovered we would just rather not. We wanted more privacy, more control over our own lives, and less involvement with so many people. Many of us came to realize just how much the one-to-one relationships we were rejecting really meant.

In my experience, the communes that worked best were structured like families. None of the communal experiments with which I had contact were able to maintain themselves, except for a group in British Columbia called The New Family. The New Family was begun by a landscape architect named Eric, his two lovers, and their children. Over time several others joined them, creating an extended family that numbered as many as twenty or thirty people. They lived on a 200-acre mountainside site in the Slocan Valley. The family grew vegetables and hay, had milk cows, and raised chickens, rabbits, and various other small animals. They fished, picked berries, and kept bees. From Eric's plans, they constructed an A-frame lodge and other buildings, using lumber from their own land. They had gardens that were works of art, as well as functional.

Eric worked just enough on landscape commissions to provide money for the things the family could not provide for itself. The group's plan was to become completely self-sufficient, in the long-run, gaining what income it needed from the sale of trees and shrubs grown on its land. This would not only provide a self-renewing source of income, but it would let The New Family live in a balanced and nondestructive relationship with the land.

The societal structure of the group was like that of a large rural family. The older of Eric's lovers filled a role similar to that of a country grandmother—she ran the mechanics of the household. The younger woman was the mother—the gentle, warm provider of love, the one who "took care of" Eric and the rest of the family. The others of the group assumed roles similar to the other members of a rural family, including the "hired hands," depending on their commitments, personalities, and skills. The family even ran its own school, managing to provide, according to the Provincial Department of Education, a program superior to any the children could find elsewhere. In The New Family, roles were defined, a structure was provided for decision making, and a vision was shared. Those who could accept its life stayed; those who could not moved on.

OPEN RELATIONSHIPS

Communes were only one of the many new lifestyles explored during the past decade. Swingers and swappers and triers of group marriage sent in their ads to underground papers like *The Free Press* every week. Then came the O'Neills and their book *Open Marriage*. It presented a view of how partners might open up their relationship, both inwardly and outwardly, in pursuit of a meaning and satisfaction not found in the traditional monogamous marriage. People such as the O'Neills and Ronald Mazur, whose book *The New Intimacy* gives an even better perspective on open relationships, have had a strong effect on contemporary thinking about marriage.

None of these alternatives, however, has worked very well. Swinging and swapping deny the emotion of jealousy. They also tend to place too much emphasis on the physical side of relationships. In swinging, the partners in a couple agree to have sexual relations with other couples without getting involved in emotional ties. They play at sex as if sex were a game—sex for the fun and variety of it. What many swingers come to realize, however, is that swinging doesn't stay so much fun. The people involved forget that it is almost impossible to share physically without having feelings about it. Swappers are couples who also want fun and variety in their sexual lives, but they seek it by switching partners. Here the people involved all know each other and intend to continue relating in ways other than sexual. Group marriages are arrangements in which three or more adults try to build a marital relationship; all involved feel and behave as though married to the rest. The tensions and strains in group marriages are probably greater than those in any of the alternatives proposed to a monogamous marital relationship.

In all of these alternatives, the physical aspect of relating is blown out of proportion. While it's good that we are learning to develop more positive feelings about our bodies, most people's needs in relationships are much more complex and deep than can be met through physical touch. In a way, sex can be the easiest part of a relationship. Our bodies know what to do, even if we are inhibited about letting them do it. Getting to know another person in depth isn't so easy. Physical contact can be both pleasant and meaningful, but if that is all that exists in a relationship it is probably an acknowledgment that the people involved don't care for each other as whole persons. If this is true, it would be difficult for them to avoid thinking of one another as mere physical objects for sensual satisfaction. Whenever this happens a relationship is robbed of its humanity and is bound to become destructive, if it is not ended.

A lot of people who experimented with new lifestyles were hurt, some permanently. Many partners who thought they would be able to encourage or even condone each other's entrance into relationships outside marriage ended up feeling demeaned or unwanted. They often discovered that they had deeper feelings about monogamy than they had suspected. Most of the experimenters, however, simply found that their experiments didn't live up to expectations.

THE MOOD TODAY

The mood of society is different today that it was when the Merry Pranksters were having so much fun. Post-Vietnam

America failed to undergo the greening that Charles Reich predicted. While we are still the world's most affluent people, our political temper has grown more conservative, a downturn in our economy has reduced our affluence, and change is viewed in a much less optimistic way than it was when we talked of "New Frontiers" and the coming of "The Great Society." We are beginning to have to face the results of a national history of overconsumption and exploitation of resources with little thought for the future. It's as though we've become mired—culturally and emotionally, as well as economically—in circumstances that have drained away our optimism and our momentum. If anything, people seem to be trying to turn back, nostalgically hoping to recreate some golden age of the past.

Turning back doesn't work, however—not even in life-styles. The circumstances of the present are not like those of other times to which we might turn for our models. But the circumstances of the present aren't as bad as they might seem, either—at least in terms of what is happening to human relationships. In fact, current economic circumstances, coupled with a sense of disappointment with the results of experiments in living styles, seem to have reinforced an interest I don't think people will ever lose: their desire for meaningful one-to-one relationships. While multitudes of relational styles are possible—and there are people for whom each seems to work—nothing can take the place of a one-to-one relationship.

This is true for me, at least. After lots of looking at, talking about, and trying on of lifestyles, I've come to realize what I intuited all along: for all the love I may have, or want to have, for many people, the only in-depth loving I have ever experienced has taken place in specially meaningful one-to-one relationships. The feeling of this love and the personal meaning of it are necessary to my life. And the same seems to be true for most of us.

2

The Return to Marriage

Some of the most exciting thinking in religious circles these days, as well as in the intellectual world in general, is that of feminists. While there is a great deal of difference among feminists when it comes to specifics, they all seem to agree on at least one thing: the post–World War II model of marriage, in which the woman is expected to be primarily a housewife and mother (even if she is working outside the home), turned out to be neither as romantic nor as satisfying as it was purported to be. Instead, for many, it turned out to be both oppressive and dehumanizing. But even if there weren't such statements being made, it is clear that marital models in which women are required to be subservient to men would be losing their legitimacy anyway. Rigid definitions of roles in marriage are oppressive for both spouses, trapping people into roles regardless of individual needs and aspirations.

ROLE OPPRESSION

There are many persons, of course, who still view marriage in traditional ways. But no one, including these people, can be so isolated that he or she does not hear the critique of marriage and the roles of men and women being made by feminists. It is being spoken too loudly and persuasively, and hits too close to important truths, to be ignored. While men and women frightened of change may be trying to hold on to some past vision, it is becoming increasingly difficult to do so.

8

Men, who have held most of the power in the modern world, know that they are vulnerable—and so do women. According to the ancient Greeks, women were able to stop wars simply by threatening to withhold their favors. Men have become much more dependent on these "favors" than they would like to admit—the love, the care, the work, of women.

While such male dependency has given women a certain kind of subtle power, the trade-off never has been equal. Men gained control over the major institutions of society and were therefore able to define the roles people should play. Since men also controlled the religious institutions of society, they were able to interpret their dominance as "God's will." So women retreated into the safe, secure roles of homemaker, child raiser, and husband "carer." Their retreat was never a completely comfortable one, however; too much of their humanity was denied.

Hints of rebellion to male oppression are scattered throughout history. In colonial America, for instance, Anne Hutchinson dared to gather men and women in her parlor in the evening to criticize the theologizing of the men ordained by the Puritans to preach the word of God. Hutchinson and women like her were persecuted for their attempts to break out of the traditional female roles, but others came along to follow their example. Finally, in the quest for the right to vote women found a cause around which to rally. The result of the Suffragist Movement was a significant, if limited, victory. Once demanding the right to vote, women found themselves demanding many other things, including the right to define their own lifestyles. The Roaring Twenties brought a taste of what liberation from traditional marital models might mean, but this didn't last. The Depression of the 30s brought with it a dampening of the free spirit of the previous decade, reinforcing traditional roles as people retreated into the protection of tight-knit family patterns. Though many women experienced another sort of coming-out as "Riveting Rosies" during World War II, most retreated into being "Sweet Suzies" when their soldier boys came home.

As we all know, a great deal has happened since then. Given the rise of the contemporary women's movement and an analogous movement among men, given the broad experiments in lifestyles that have taken place during the past decade, given the large numbers of women turning to work outside the home, and given the invasion by women of almost all of the areas from which they were previously excluded—given all these factors, there is no way for marital roles of the past to remain unchallenged.

This challenge is as important to men as it is to women, important in a positive sense. Men have as much need to be freed from the oppression of rigid roles as do women. Most men have endured a lifetime of conditioning—to be strong, to be aggressive and winning, to take on responsibility for providing, and to excel, as demonstrated by the gaining of wealth, power, and prestige. Men have been conditioned to dominate women and children, a heavy burden to bear.

Men need to be able to share more fully with women the burdens they have assumed; they need to be able to see positive images of themselves in other than traditional male roles. Men lag far behind women in demanding that this be done, even though the beginnings of a male equivalent of the current women's movement have arisen. Not only does "house-husband" still seem like an odd word, but few men have dared to think of what it might mean not to be the wage earner, and all of the other things commonly associated with being a good husband. Even in the world of work outside the home, though men may grudgingly be accepting women as co-workers in traditionally male fields, few men are moving into fields up until now dominated by women, such as clerical work and nursing. And when men do enter fields having to do with traditionally female interests, such as interior decorating, fashion design, or hairdressing, they are often typed as effeminate, if not gay. Men have to do a lot of shucking off and restructuring of their self-image if they are to get their own liberation in order.

MEETING ON FREE GROUND

But suppose this happens—suppose that free men and free women could meet each other on equal ground. What kind of relationships would they have, assuming, as I think we can, that they would want to relate? Clues to this abound in the subtle kind of shifts now taking place in patterns of courtship, marriage, and family relationships. People are becoming less frantic about the first, more open to possibilities in the second, and more flexible and sensitive to the third.

The role of courtship (or whatever it is that happens these days before marriage) has changed significantly in our society. Today it is not only becoming acceptable to be a single adult, but it is becoming all right to remain an uncommitted one. Marriage used to be the primary goal of most single adults' relational lives. Now that this is no longer so, single people are free to initiate relationships without any preconditions and without needing to play either the role of the pursuer or the pursued in a courtship game. To the degree that individuals can live as they really are, without having to feel they ought to be something or someone else, they should be able to build firmer, more satisfying, and more lasting relationships.

As for marriage, the institution is far from dead, although there is a significant shift taking place in our understanding of how it should begin and our responsibility for what becomes of it. More and more couples have come to view their weddings as an affirmation and celebration of an existing reality rather than as a sanctioning of a special kind of new relationship. Rather than dying, the institutions of marriage and the family are broadening and becoming redefined in ways that better meet the needs of the freer and more liberated individuals within them. The one need that has not seemed to change, the one constant on which any good, workable marriage has always had to be based, is that of maintaining a committed, central relationship with another person—a person with whom a depth of love and respect is uniquely shared.

When two people become close, their knowledge of, delight and interest in, and concern for each other's unique personhood is most important. Such an attitude must be present in any relationship if it is to be meaningfully intimate. This allows each person the freedom to be herself or himself without having to worry about what is the proper *role* to be playing, or what is the polite or ballsy (or "ovarian") thing to do. Life is complicated, and the decisions that have to be made in life are equally complicated, including our decisions about how best to be ourselves as the men and women we want to be. About our gender we have no choice. About how we realize our personhood, within and without relationships like marriage, we have a great deal of choice.

We should try to gain more and more freedom, both in society and within ourselves, to make our choices in ways that will allow us to be as creative, loving, useful, and satisfying to ourselves and others as is possible. If we can live out our freedom in such a way we are bound to develop a greater respect for and valuing of not only our own gender, but also our co-equals of the opposite sex. The kind of elitism and domination sought by chauvinists of either sex is something we must reject if there is to be true freedom for any of us. If we are to be free to be ourselves as we really are and want to be, if we are to be able to bring about a true sharing of selves with both men and women, then both elitism and domination must be done away with and new models for relationships found.

As I have suggested, this is beginning to happen. Even people in traditional marriages are opening the doors on their relationships and are seeking to redefine them in more satisfying ways. Both men and women are saying that if they cannot find fulfillment as individuals within their marriages, then to hell with them. They are being helped to say this because both divorce and single adulthood are turning into acceptable options as they become more common. Whereas society used to strongly condemn divorce, and single adults (especially women) were regarded as somehow incomplete, this is no longer so. In many environments, such as my own church, there are easily as many unmarried as married adults. While there are problems unique to a single adult or to a divorced person, such problems no longer need be seen as overpowering. In fact, many people are beginning to question whether marriage really does have any advantages for them.

THE QUESTION OF MARRIAGE

The answer to this question varies from person to person, but my experience, both as a minister and a counselor, suggests that marriage has not lost its appeal. While for some people being or becoming unmarried may be a better alternative than being or becoming married, marriage is and is likely to remain the preferred choice for most of us. We have found and will continue to find that there is neither an easier nor a happier way to live as an adult.

This is an opinion, of course, and it could be wrong, but my opinion is not uninformed. Recent statistics show that I am not the only minister being swamped with requests for weddings; they far outweigh, these days, the requests for marital counseling. Every year of my professional life, I have officiated at dozens of weddings. This hasn't changed. What has changed, however, are the circumstances under which people are coming to see me.

It is no longer unusual for a couple to tell me they are living together when we begin to talk about a wedding. More often than not, however, the couple has come to the decision to marry because the individuals sincerely want to, not because they feel a wedding would be "right." Certainly many couples still receive their share of social or family pressures—there is a remnant of obligation in even the most enlightened couple's decision to be wed. But what is important is that feelings of obligation are seldom, now, a determining factor in the initiation of a marriage. With the availability of birth control methods and relatively easy access to abortion, even "shotgun weddings" are becoming things of the past. We get shotgun abortions now.

An example of the typical couple coming to see me these days is John and Jo. John had finished college and gone into the Peace Corps. Jo had been an art major who dropped out of school and became involved in the civil rights and peace movements. After disillusionment, drugs, and a bit of street scene experience, Jo found herself living communally in a house with a number of other people—including John, who was back in school studying social work. It did not take them long to find that they were attracted to each other and that the loose structure of communal living was unsatisfying to them, so they moved out and took an apartment of their own. They then decided to make a complete break from the past and "buy a place in the country." While it was clear that they would never make any money at farming, they enjoyed the life they had together and began to feel that they were more than just two people living together. They had become a family of sorts, and even began to have thoughts of having a child. In my mind, it was with this consciousness that their marriage had begun. All that was left to do was to celebrate the choice.

MAKING THE CHOICE

The story of Jo and John may seem a bit romantic, I admit, but I have met many couples whose experience is similar to theirs. It illustrates a trend that is becoming more and more common. Many couples today seem to be moving toward marriage through stages, feeling little compulsion to jump from one stage to another. Relations can remain casual or they can progress to an open sharing of intimacy, or they can move to what Margaret Mead calls "an arrangement," in which a couple agrees to live as husband and wife but without any legal commitment. A couple can move through all of these stages without feeling the need to have the clergy or law grant them the right to live together openly without harassment. This allows the step to marriage to be taken for its own sake, as is preferable, rather than for the gain of marital privileges. A couple can thus decide to be wed because they have *chosen* to be married—because they find they like living in the state of marriage with all the commitment it implies. Then, and only then, is it time to celebrate the choice and affirm the commitment—to have a wedding.

Before talking more about this choice, though, something should be said about an alternative suggested a few years ago by a Unitarian colleague of mine. Even though he had picked up the idea from *Marriage and Morals* by Bertrand Russell, written over fifty years ago, it received a lot of national publicity. What Russell had suggested, and what my colleague re-proposed, was that we ought to sanction trial marriages for young people who want to see what married life is like before committing themselves to a permanent relationship.

This is an intriguing idea. However, the trouble with trial marriage, as Margaret Mead has pointed out, is that we cannot *try* marriage. We cannot find out what marriage is like unless we risk it, including risking the full commitment required.

The idea of trial marriage is merely a diversion, anyway. We do not need to devise new legal or quasi-legal forms of pre-marital cohabitation. Instead we need to relax, and allow a quite natural form that has evolved among us—a movement from casual to committed relationships, and a *de facto* state of marriage—to continue without feeling a need to moralize or disapprove of it because it does not fit a traditional model. If we can be more relaxed about people living together, the marriages that result are bound to be more stable and happier than those sanctioned only by the proper words of a member of the clergy or the law.

3

New Models

Many of us were brought up with a "picture-book" notion of what marriage ought to be like. This kind of marriage was held out as an ideal in Sunday school, in school textbooks, and by our parents and their friends. It was the kind of marriage once exemplified in the movie *Cheaper by the Dozen*, and now pictured in Disney film after Disney film starring good old Fred MacMurray.

This "picture-book" marriage was the clean, wholesome one, typical of nice, home-owning suburban folk who took seriously the traditional vow "to have and to hold from this day forward", no matter what. The trouble is, I have yet to meet any married couple who has found this picture-book ideal satisfactory for dealing with all the "no matter whats" it has had to face.

PROBLEMS WITH THE PICTURE-BOOK IDEAL

This picture-book ideal is just that—an ideal, one not only difficult to attain, but wholly inadequate for meeting the real-life crises that must be dealt with by any married couple. The ideal is too confining, since it assumes that a couple and the family they create can be self-sustaining. In a picture-book marriage the couple is expected to be able to supply itself with whatever resources it needs. Kindness and friendship can be shared with friends, neighbors, and relatives, but

16

real intimacy must be kept within the confines of the family; a committed and loving couple is expected to be able to provide each other with whatever intimacy either needs. Outside one's work and neighborhood, all of a person's relational needs are supposed to be met within his or her own marriage and family.

It should not take the increasing divorce rate of recent years to show that such an ideal of marriage is not working. Anyone involved in counseling, or even anyone who looks closely at his neighbors, can see the gap between our expectations about "the loving and cherishing for better or for worse" of the traditional wedding vow and the realities of most people's marital lives. Trying to live up to the heavy demands of an exclusively monogamous, self-contained style of marriage, when such an ideal is unworkable for a couple, causes great pain, frustration, and psychological harm to all involved.

Many who experience the gap between the expectation and reality of marriage decide to endure their discomfort. Others turn from the conflict with indifference or hostility. Some turn to outside interests. A few try to explore and resolve their problems in a healthier way, attempting to create a whole new pattern for their relationships.

DENIAL

One of the simplest things for a couple to do, however, is to deny that a problem exists. These couples for whom picture-book marriage is only a pretense are in trouble. The typical denying husband and wife expend tremendous energy in trying to appear as though their marriage is ideal. Generally they are good actors, and that is why we are shocked when we learn that they are getting divorced. "They *seemed* so happy," we say. They "seemed so happy" because they had learned how to perform so well in public that their conflicts would be hidden. Such a performance has a cost, however. It takes a lot of psychic energy to pretend to be calm, controlled, and happy when you are not. This makes it all the harder to deal with feelings when they finally do break out into the open.

In her book about the years of her marriage, *From Time to Time*, Hannah Tillich describes how Paul, her otherwise brilliant husband, consistently refused to admit that he was intimately involved with anyone else even when "caught" at it. When confronted, Tillich was never able to do anything but break down and cry until Hannah would leave him alone and he could rebuild his façade.

In a situation such as this, a common defense is to dissociate from one's behavior and repress the unpleasant feelings that go with it (and I suspect this is what Paul Tillich did). Unfortunately, the energy that goes with feelings, especially negative ones, does not dissipate when they are repressed. If feelings are repressed long enough, the energy associated with them will build to the point where it has to break loose. This breaking out is often unpredictable, frequently destructive. It may be difficult for a couple to deal with the power of repressed feelings when they finally do erupt, because the outbreak is likely to evoke an equally destructive response. Once long-repressed feelings are loose, partners may be unable to refrain from lashing out at each other or at innocent bystanders, such as children or friends. Once hurt, many people find themselves trying to create comparable hurt in others. Alternatively, they may try to cut off from their feelings altogether and become withdrawn, cold, and mechanical. If either of these patterns goes on very long within a marriage, the chances for a continuing, fruitful relationship may be lost; and divorce may become the only remaining solution. Ending a disintegrated relationship with divorce would, at least, be more care-full than to maintain its destructiveness.

CHEATING

Even though acceptance of divorce has increased in our society, couples in trouble often search for other alternatives. Rather than split up a marriage some unsatisfied spouses turn to outside relationships for fulfillment—relationships with jobs or other interests or other people. (During my first marriage I often jokingly said that the church had become my mistress. It turned out to be more unjokingly true than I had suspected.)

Clearly the outside interest that is most explosive is the extramarital lover. Having an affair is the classic response of a dissatisfied husband or wife. Studies show that over half of all marriages have had at least one spouse involved in an extramarital sexual relationship. If we were to add to these all of the other intimate, though not overtly sexual, relationships engaged in by spouses outside of their marriages, it would be clear that the vast majority of married people need and seek meaningful personal relationships with people other than their spouses.

Such relationships do not have to involve deception, but they usually do. This is because the "cheating" spouse believes his or her partner will see the outside relationship as a sign of disrespect or a lack of love—both of which may be closer to the truth than the "offending" spouse would like to admit. The clandestine nature of affairs makes them, potentially, very dangerous. The cheating is usually discovered or made known in some way. Spouses may even want to get caught. When this happens the offended partner is bound to feel unloved and devalued, and the offender is bound to feel guilty and confused. The very nature of cheating harms both the self-respect of the one doing it and the one cheated upon. Yet, given the way people expect their spouses to respond, and given the high ideal of conduct (meaning fidelity) they assume society expects, those who find themselves needing or wanting intimate extramarital relationships can seldom conceive of any other way to satisfy their needs and desires other than through deception.

OTHER MANEUVERS

Of course another way to respond to a less-than-satisfying marriage is to simply go on living together in an increasingly destructive way. Some couples seem able to tolerate, even enjoy, tearing each other apart. I have counseled with couples who have lived this way for thirty years or more! While people may be able to find a certain amount of satisfaction in destroying each other, this is hardly the sort of satisfaction that justifies a couple's staying together. Certainly partners who cannot resolve conflicts are better off separated. If people don't soar when they leap off the cliff into marriage, and if they have not provided themselves with parachutes, they had better reach out and grab hold of whatever branches they can find sticking out of the side of the cliff.

All of this sounds rather scary, I admit. It is not at all the sort of thing one would want to celebrate in the kind of weddings I will describe. But these days, people do seem to be growing more realistic about what to expect in marriage. The gap between expectation and reality is getting smaller. Not to marry is an acceptable option in our society as it is redefining itself today; so is divorce. For this reason marriage is being seen less and less often as cliff jumping. Serial marriage, as it is called, is gaining a kind of respectability.

Margaret Mead has suggested that rather than do away with marriage conceived of as primarily a one-to-one relationship, we should break it up into a series, since the needs we have as spouses vary as we progress through life. One's first marriage would be for learning about sex and romance. Those needing the learning would be young men and young women. Those needing the romance, having completed their learning, would be older women and older men. In between one's early and late marriages would be marriage for the conception of children and the raising of families. Finally, late in life would come marriage for companionship. Although I heard Dr. Mead say these things in a private seminar, her own life description in *Blackberry Winter* shows that she was not reluctant to follow out at least part of this model in her own life. The unfortunate thing about divorce and remarriage is that it is seldom so well calibrated as the above suggests. Though divorce solves the problem of an unsatisfying relationship, it usually does nothing to ensure that the needs of either spouse will be any better met in a future relationship. It has been my experience that divorced people, all too often, fall back into making the same kind of mistakes in their new marriages that they made in the old ones.

CENTERING

But no matter how many mistakes we may make, the pull toward marriage, whether the first or the fourth, remains strong. There is a pull toward a relationship with another person in which will exist love, affection, respect, and support. There is a pull toward a relationship with someone else who can be at the center of one's life.

This idea of centering is the best I have found to describe what I believe to be the most workable and satisfying model for marriage today. The model I would like to suggest is one flexible enough to meet a couple's varying desires, open enough to eliminate the need for deception, and realistic enough to allow the individuals to respect each other's needs and desires for meaningful relationships outside marriage. At the same time, it recognizes and values the need for a centered relationship with a spouse.

The Bible speaks of the most intimate kind of relationship possible as "knowing." To know someone is not just to share something like sex; it is to be deeply and intimately involved at all levels. It requires a unique kind of intimacy that will allow a couple to search and grow together, to reveal and be revealed to in all honesty and depth, affirming each other's wholeness. The question is: with how many people can we share such a "knowing" at any one time?

Even after all of the recent experimenting with communal life and group marriage in our society, there seems to be a growing feeling that "knowing" happens best in one-to-one relationships. People involved in communes, such as the one I visited in British Columbia, usually end up pairing off. Though the pairings may be temporary, commune members seem to do it so they can have at least one person with whom they can share a depth of intimacy impossible with the group as a whole. It is as though people are spiderwebs whose strands reach out in many directions at once. In most of our relationships we are connected to others by only a few strands at one time because the connections are so far from our centers. There seems to be a need to get closer to a special someone so that many strands can be interconnected with that person. What this means is that people have two very different sorts of relational needs. Centered and noncentered relationships are both important for the development of one's full personhood.

The people living in the communal situations I have observed have worked out all sorts of patterns for relating. Some have succeeded better than others. None, however, has found a way of being free from the obligation of acting responsibly and caring for another. New lifestyles do not free people from the need for caring about the quality of their relationships if they want to go on living together. New lifestyles do not provide a warrant for uncaring behavior. The ethics of interpersonal relationships remain the same, whether the people living together are in traditional marriage or in the extended family of a commune.

MULTIPLE RELATIONSHIPS

What the experiments of the recent past have shown is that few of us are ready for a life of multicentered intimacy. The demands of multiple caring and the dynamics of multiple sharing become too much to bear. It is much more difficult to achieve a stable and deeply intimate relationship with several people than it is with one other.

Group marriage of the variety talked about in Robert Rimmer's book, *Proposition 31*, in which two couples merge their families into one and share with each other in everything, including their sexual lives, may seem like an attractive alternative to some. But there is more idealism and naïveté in believing that such genuinely multicentered, multiloving relationships can succeed than there is even in the picture-book concept of a single-couple marriage. To make a multi-centered relationship work all of the people entering into it must share not only an equal commitment to the relationship but an equal love and respect for each other. Not only does this seem unlikely, but I have doubts as to whether the depth achieved in the relationships would match the depth possible for two partners who choose to center their relational lives.

There are people who do not need or desire such centered relationships, who prefer to stop short of the knowing I have mentioned. Most of us, though, seek to be involved with some *one* else in a way that is consistent, predictable, responsive, and affirming. Without such a relationship we feel incomplete—something less than the whole persons we would like to be.

No one person can fully meet another's needs and desires, however. No one personality can ever fully satisfy another. Unless two people can enter into a relationship assuming that they cannot and should not be all things to each other, they are compounding the risks of a marriage. Much of what is within us we want to share with the person we choose to know best—and we do so. But some things are better shared with others. This is not a defect. It follows from our humanness. To be fully human we have to be *both* centered and multirelational at the same time.

There is danger in such an assumption, of course. Relating to others is often done at the expense of one's centered relationship. It is only when other relationships *add* to one's life—to the wholeness to be shared in the centered relationship—that these relationships should be risked.

It is also dangerous to assume that multirelationships can be a cure for a central one that has ceased to be fulfilling. This doesn't work—as I found out in my own life. When the marriage I had begun "prematurely" at nineteen was in trouble, and the conventional remedies had not helped, I thought the marriage could be saved by turning to other relationships.

But rather than enrich my centered relationship, this action proved to me that the centering I had had with my wife was gone. Much was holding us together, like our children, financial obligations, and fear of the reaction of others; but none of these things had to do with the love, respect, and affirmation necessary for maintaining a centered relationship.

THE MARRIAGE POTENTIAL

I believe that the multirelational, yet centered, model I have described is the best alternative to the picture-book ideal of marriage that has become unworkable for so many. The model I have suggested is one that works for my wife Jan and me, and it can work for others. It works because it allows a couple to interact with other people in a non-threatening way, making unnecessary cheating, promiscuity, the repeated mistakes of serial marriage, or the loneliness of having no one with whom to be close. It provides a way for a couple to share with other people at the same time the individuals remain committed to building and nourishing their relationship with each other. Building a centered but multirelational life is a way of adding dimensions to life impossible otherwise and of avoiding the pain of deception or the denial and defeat of an unworkable marriage.

The experiments of the 60s opened up the whole question of what is the ideal marriage; the women's movement which followed brought into question the traditional roles within marriage. The result has not been a doing away with people's desire for the kind of centered relationship that grows into marriage. Instead, the result has been rethinking the model of marriage.

Has the picture-book ideal failed? For growing numbers of people, yes. But this does not mean that marriage based on a centered and committed relationship of two people has become an anachronism. What has happened is that our models of what marriage should be have opened up. We have been freed to rethink what such an institution can mean to us. This lets marriage be something we can take advantage of, rather than something that restricts us. As Herbert Otto, one of America's outstanding marriage counseling experts, puts it, now that the institution has been freed from cultural restrictions, every marriage has within it the possibility for *greater* commitment, communication, love, understanding, warmth, joy, and growth. Working to make these possibilities real is goal enough for any centered relationship. If this can happen, marriage or whatever other form of union a couple might choose is well worth the celebration of a wedding, for the wedding has become, in itself, a celebration of life.

4

Celebrating the Choice

One of the many things a minister does is officiate at weddings. It comes with the robe of authority that goes with ordination and the notion that a minister is a representative of the community. In my case, I doubt if there is any other thing I do that fills more time. Whether it is because people like the liberal approach of the church I serve or because of my attitude that a couple should "own" their wedding, writing and creating as much of it as they can, seldom a week goes by without my taking part in a ceremony. (This used to confuse the heck out of my children when their mother would tell them that their dad wasn't home because he was off "marrying" someone again!) ·

RESPONSIBILITY FOR A WEDDING

I like the involvement I have with people who want to be wed. It is a chance to see people when they are happy and at their best—something not all that usual for a minister, who spends much of his time dealing with people in crisis. I enjoy sharing in the good feelings and commitment of a couple at the time of their wedding, and I am enough of a traditionalist to see the importance of not only giving a couple a chance to express the meaning of their marriage in a way suitable to themselves, but also of conveying to them something of the responsibilities and implications of their choice.

Presenting such an attitude to a couple who wants to marry seems to have a positive impact on them. Out of our interchange comes a mutual sharing of respect which adds a great deal to the meaning of the wedding itself. It ends up with no one feeling shoved through someone else's agenda. The following letter that I received from one couple expresses this feeling:

We wish to keep our wedding simple and direct. But by simple we mean more than just short or straight-to-the-point. We feel that a wedding is more than just a formal agreement between two people—more than just a tradition for maintaining an ethic or a moral position. It is as if a wedding is an expression of faith not just between a husband and a wife, but one which announces a faith in human beings and their community. A wedding is an act which holds the future anew—and embraces the past. Our wedding is a ritual which embraces human history and life—one in which a new family arises amongst the community—a new body on which to build. At the same time, our wedding reaffirms the past—confirms the meaning of life that has gone before in the rebirth it gives.

We have chosen you to wear the coat of the community—to act as a symbol for human beings and their relationships, to whom we announce and celebrate our union. We come before you to fulfill this task. We leave you to do your part.

I must admit that I was not altogether comfortable with the couple's charge. It is one thing to feel good about a couple's choice and to share in the celebration of its meaning. It is quite another to be asked to be an agent of the community in the sanctioning and sanctifying of a marriage, when the community itself seems so unsure about the meaning of marriage.

THE TRADITIONAL VIEW

Seventeen years ago when it was my turn to go through the process for the first time, there was no question about what a wedding was for—a wedding was the way one got married. My fiancée and I would never have thought of living together out of wedlock, and it had taken us six years to work through the stages of puppy love, romance, breaking up, rediscovery, courtship, and engagement. Finally the time came when, whether we were ready for it or not, the only thing our hearts, heads, and hormones would let us do was to take the "till death do us part" leap off the cliff into marriage.

The price we knowingly paid for the privileges granted by marriage (the right to relate to one another without any social restraints) was the promise to stand by each other forever and to resist the temptation to know anyone else in a depth comparable to what we shared. The giving up of attention paid to and by others was a sacrifice we thought we would be willing to make as an expression of our love. Our wedding was the time when we made a moral and legal commitment to maintain a life together forever, no matter what. I promised, in the words of the traditional wedding vow, to take the woman I was marrying:

. . . to be my wedded wife, to live together with you in the holy state of matrimony. I promise to love you, comfort you, honor and keep you, in sickness and in health, for richer or poorer; and, forsaking all others, keep myself only unto you, as long as we both shall live.

The meaning and intent of this promise was certain. Our ability to live up to it was something else. But when we shared our vow we really meant it; the "till death do us part" pledge was the only way we felt we could express the fullness of our love. Our parents were suburban, Republican, conventional. We cared about them and their feelings and were conditioned to approach things in their footsteps. This meant placing ourselves in the hands of our parents, an Episcopal priest, and Emily Post, when it came time to plan for a wedding.

The scene was familiar enough. My wife-to-be and I had secretly climaxed our courtship with a "will you—oh, yes" one cold winter night in New Hampshire. The following Christmas, after a very heavy summer of romance, I asked my brother if he would take me to a wholesale jeweler to buy a ring. I bought the ring and presented it in a properly timed surprise, so that it could be brought home that night and shown the parents. I think I even did the polite thing of asking my fiancée's father for permission to marry her. (Men still thought of women as property then.) The engagement was to be a long one, but it became increasingly difficult for us to curb our libidos and to continue the fiction of a genteel courtship when the activities on the living room couch made going home to separate beds seem ridiculous. So we set a late summer date for an ornate church wedding, sent out hundreds of invitations, let the parents arrange a proper country-club reception, waded through showers and bachelor parties, got together the formal clothes and wedding dress, hired a photographer, and set up an interview with the minister.

All of this was undertaken without any question. It was the way things were supposed to be done. But from the time I met the minister and was told what we would have to do, I was hostile to the process. I hated every moment of our wedding. It seemed ironically appropriate to the agony of the whole scene that the organ broke down just before the ceremony was to begin and the bride had to click down the aisle in silence and tears after forty-five minutes of trying to get the damn thing going.

THE VIEW TODAY

In one way or another, so go most conventional weddings. People place themselves in the hands of others to be manipulated through a ceremony whose form and content have little meaning for them. The couple whose letter I quoted earlier felt free of this manipulation, which is good. I could never knowingly advocate to others the kinds of things that put my former wife and me through such misery when we were preparing for our wedding. Part of the responsibility I feel to that memory has prompted me to offer to couples an alternative. The reward for me is that then I can be a part of something creative, rather than a caricature of a potted palm.

I believe it is important that there be ministers, representing, as they do, the sensitivity and ultimacy of religious concern, who are willing to respond to a couple's desire to make its own wedding. When a couple comes to see me about a wedding, I explain to them that I do not believe my words can create a marriage for them. Nothing I can say or do as a minister, even when I also act as an agent of the state, can guarantee the health or endurance of a relationship. There is no magic in the words of a wedding ceremony, even though traditional services may pretend that there is. It is far better to let the words and form of a ceremony place the responsibility for the success of a wedding where it belongs—directly on the couple. The words of one recent ceremony in which I took part express this idea very well:

As the years go by you will realize that this marriage you have chosen for yourselves was not given to you by anyone else. It has been, and must continue to be, a process that builds throughout your lives. You must work at it day by day, meeting the disappointments, as well as the joys, that your lives together will bring.

We have gathered with you this evening to help you give added life to this marriage that you have chosen for yourselves. But, in doing this, we realize that this outward act is but a symbol of that which is inward and real: a union of two people, which a church may bless and the state may make legal, but which neither church nor state can create or annul. It is such a union, by your own free choice—and with full knowledge of what that choice means—that you two have come to live.

In such a context, the choice to join cannot be regarded as an incidental decision. Such a vow does not represent an exercise in cliff-jumping, nor does it cut off other possibilities for relationships or commit the couple to continue a marriage after love dies or after the relationship becomes destructive. But it does affirm that the couple feels sure about the depth of their love, their respect for each other, and their trust in the future. This is the sentiment of the Hindu vow which is often used in weddings at which I officiate:

I,——, take you, ——, to be the husband of my days,
To be the father of our children, to be the companion of my home.
We shall keep together what share of sorrow our lives may lay upon us,
And we shall hold together our store of goodness and of love.
   Take this ring, freely, as a token of my love and as a symbol of my
intention to live with you in love and respect.

Such a statement is an expression of *intention*. It is appropriate in a situation in which a wedding is seen as both a
ceremony of a couple's *public commitment* to live together as husband and wife and a *celebration* of their happiness and joy
about it. The couple to be wed, rather than just going on
living together, is able, in such a setting, to reinforce what
their relationship means and to express their happiness about
it to those they invite to share the moment.

A wedding should not be seen as a licensing of marital
privileges. Instead it should be seen as a celebration of a transition from an open-ended, testing relationship to one based
on sureness about the future continuation of a couple's depth
of love and understanding. Celebrating this is an appropriate
way to launch into what, in the Jewish tradition, is called "the
spending and fruitfulness of many days."

OWNING YOUR WEDDING

Couples should be given the freedom to create their own
ceremony. It is perhaps easier for me than for some other
ministers to give a couple such freedom because the religious
movement of which I am a part values freedom and honestly
believes individuals are responsible for their own behavior.
But the point of view I am expressing is shared by the clergy
in a growing number of other churches and synagogues.

When a couple approaches me about a wedding I explain
my attitude about marriage and weddings to them. If they are
comfortable with it I then invite them to look at examples of
wedding ceremonies authored by other couples, take them
home, read them, and then come back with an idea of what
they would like to do. While I particularly delight in a fresh

approach, all I really want to be sure of is that the couple "owns" the ceremony—that they take responsibility for it, just as they must take responsibility for their marriage. I am not interested in taking part in a wedding which a couple does not take seriously enough to want to work on themselves. If they simply wish a marriage legalized, I can sign the papers for them without having to go through the sham of a ceremony. If a couple wants the pretense of a ceremony without taking any responsibility for it they are always free to find a judge willing to perform a civil ceremony or to go to another minister. But if a couple wishes their wedding to be their own, I am willing to do almost anything with them, as long as it doesn't compromise my taste or beliefs—something I have seldom been asked to do.

An example of the sort of thing I have been willing to do took place on a farm several miles out in the country. The couple to be wed were theater people who were working in the city trying to save up enough money to build a house on the farm so they could begin to work the land. I had not known the couple long; they were not members of my church. They were part of the larger community that has little need for formal worship and does not want to belong to an organized religious group. But, church-going or not, they still wanted a chance to celebrate their decision to be married. I felt it important to help make this possible for them and to share in a ceremony in the *only* appropriate place for them— the hillside on which their future was going to be lived.

It is important, I believe, for there to be ministers "vested" with the authority of the state who are willing to say it does not matter if neither member of a couple goes to church; to say it does not matter if one of them is Jewish and the other Lutheran, or that one of them has been divorced, or that they have been openly living together. It is important that there be clergy willing to recognize the seriousness of intent, the *religiousness*, of people even when they do not want God preached at them, even when they say they don't believe in God. It is important that there be representatives of communities of faith who are willing to join a couple in affirming their commitment and celebrating their choice no matter whether it is done with organ music, folk songs, or jazz; no matter whether the words used are traditional or informal; no matter whether the wedding takes place in an open field or in a church. It is important that there be ministers, priests, and rabbis who do not care whether brides are given away, whether formal clothes are worn, whether any of the forms of traditional weddings are observed. There need to be, and there are, religious professionals willing to respond to a couple in their uniqueness, rather than trying to force them through forms invented for others, or done for others' sakes.

GAY COUPLES

Responding to people in their uniqueness can include the fact that the couple is not heterosexual. Many gay couples share the same kind of love and commitment as do their straight brothers and sisters. If such a couple comes to me I ask them the same kinds of questions and use the same approach to creating a wedding as I would for any other couple. I have been disappointed a few times in my experience with gay couples. Some of their weddings have turned out to be masquerades, something a part of the gay spectrum. But I have to admit that I have sometimes misjudged straight couples, too.

I believe that gay couples who wish to live openly in a committed relationship are just as "married" as straight couples in the same circumstances. I also feel that they are entitled to celebrate this fact and to have it recognized in a church, such as mine, which believes that it is the quality of love, respect, and commitment in a relationship that matters, not the gender of the partners. I only wish more gay people could feel secure enough and society could become open enough for gay men and women to be able to live their lifestyles openly, and to be able to celebrate the love and commitment of their relationships.

Of course, there is nothing legal about the gay weddings in

which I take part. The legal rights and protections of formal marriages, such as they are, are not yet available to gay couples. To provide legal protections for their relationships they now have to enter into special agreements about property, inheritance, and whatever else it is they want to protect. The irony is, given the current nature of the Internal Revenue Codes, drawing up special precise agreements rather than signing a general marriage contract does not sound like such a bad idea.

THE LAW

Anyone who has gone through a divorce realizes that the specific rights of the parties depend on their particular circumstances: the presence or lack of children, their jobs (or lack of them) and income levels, arrangements they have made about property ownership, other documents such as wills, and the astuteness of their lawyers (or the whim of a judge). It makes a lot of sense, whether they are going to be legally married or not, for a couple to draw up a contract defining their rights and obligations as a couple. Many people are now doing this.

A few people are also deciding to celebrate marriage without taking the added step of legalizing it. I share in such weddings because I believe that a marriage is legitimized by its intention, rather than by signing papers. For all the years I have been in the ministry, from the time of the first wedding in which I ever took part (as a student minister unable to sign a license as an agent of the state), I have separated the legal proceeding—the signing of the marriage certificate—from the celebrating of the wedding.

Mine is an old-fashioned point of view, actually. In medieval times civil and canon law were separated. Under civil law, a woman was regarded as a piece of property whose possession could be transferred from one man to another. A wedding was a sacrament in which two people were joined together in marriage.

The legal and sacramental aspects of marriage have been put together in the United States. Members of the clergy here are licensed to act as agents of the state as well as representatives of their religious groups, but in most countries of the world the legal and sacramental aspects of marriage have been kept separate. From the standpoint of both history and a global perspective, then, there is nothing unusual about a wedding without a license. I wish more people who have philosophical objections to the involvement of the state in their relationships would understand this. All too many people slip into living arrangements only half-heartedly appreciating what their relationship means. They live without commitment, missing the enrichment that is possible only when such a commitment is made and affirmed in a public way.

THE INTENTION OF MARRIAGE

The depth of a couple's feelings for one another is worth celebrating, and their intention can be reinforced and made more meaningful by expressing it in public. For this reason I have no doubt about the value of weddings—as long as they are expressive of what couples intend their relationships to be, and the couples are willing to take responsibility for what happens. Sanctioning this sort of wedding is one way a church and its minister can say yes to the uniqueness and worth of the people who come to them. Weddings cannot *make* a marriage, but they can add to a good beginning—and such an addition is justification enough.

I began this chapter by describing how I first approached the beginning of marriage. My assumption was that it was "until death do us part" no matter what happened. As my ministry went along and I became more in touch with the pains and joys of others, it became clear that a major source of unhappiness for people lay in their maintaining this same assumption about the demand of their wedding vow: "to love and to cherish, in *sickness* or in health . . . till death do us part." This is a beautiful intention, but sometimes the sickness of a marriage cannot be cured—better put, often the restriction and pain of the people involved cannot be cured within the marriage and it is better, for the sake of those involved, to endure the lesser discomfort of having the marriage dissolved.

Because this is true, it seems to me that the *intention* of the Hindu vow quoted previously is a better way of stating a good beginning for a marriage. Perhaps even better is the rewording of the traditional vow now frequently used: "I take you to be my wedded wife/husband . . . to live and be with as long as love lasts." If love or happiness has left a relationship, if a relationship is sick beyond curing, then it may be that the only caring thing that can be done is to change it—to have it stop being a marriage. It's good to take a parachute along when jumping off a cliff.

With all this in mind, perhaps the best way to begin marriage would be in the spirit of the words of Walt Whitman who said, and I paraphrase one of his poems as it was used in a wedding:

> Listen, I will be honest with you.
> I do not offer the old smooth prizes,
> But rough new ones . . .
>
> Afoot and lighthearted, take to the open road,
> Healthy, free, the world before you,
> The long brown path before you,
> Leading wherever you choose . . .
>
> Camerado, I give you my hand!
> I give you my love more precious than money,
> I give you myself before preaching or law;
> Will you give me yourself?
> Will you come travel with me?
> Shall we stick by each other as long as we live?

To which the free spirits among my couples add:

> . . . not "live"—"love."

If a couple can enter into marriage, conceiving of it as a freely chosen adventure capable of enhancing their individual lives, we should delight in celebrating a wedding with them whether it is until death do they part or not.

5

Romance Is Not Enough

It is impossible to be truly human without having personal relationships—relationships which are different from the sexual or defensive pairing of other species. Without them we would have no language, no sharing of experience, no sense of community, no consciousness. Memory, intellect, feelings, and ideas all depend on an interaction with others. Not only do our consciousnesses and personalities develop out of contact with others, but achieving a fullness of personhood depends on having relationships in which there is intimacy and depth. As Martin Buber puts it, although most of our interactions are objective and without great feeling—that is, we treat most things as *Its*—the person who lives only with *Its* is not fully human. To be human in the fullest sense we've got to move beyond "Itiness" and achieve the kinds of relationships with others in which it is appropriate to use the most personal of pronouns, addressing the other as "Thou." We cannot even experience *ourselves* in depth without the learning that comes from sharing in depth with someone else. For this reason, the classic biblical phrase, "Love thy neighbor as thyself" links other-love and self-love. If we can fully know someone else, and if such a relationship can be mutual, out of this interaction can come full love and respect of self and others, without which it is difficult to imagine being *humanly* alive.

GROUP EXPERIENCES

With the demise of traditional models, such as the romance, courtship, and marriage ideal of the past, many people seem to have been left floundering in their search for interpersonal relationships. Out of this floundering have come all of the recent experimentation in lifestyles and the rise of the small group as a new model for interpersonal salvation. In small-group settings people have sought the fullness and depth of interpersonal relationships otherwise missing from their lives. For many, these groups have added new dimensions and insights. Though horror stories are told about the cans-of-worms opened by T-groups, the wrecked marriages due to communal experiments, and the problems created when spouses try to relate to a lot of people with openness and honesty, most group experiences do turn out to be healthy and therapeutic for the people involved. Group experiences provide at least one way of achieving some sense of community in our otherwise alienating urban environment.

The experiences possible within a trusting and caring circle of people can be of tremendous value to a person, but they seldom can take the place of the centered relationship. No one knows this better than those who bounce from one group experience to another, seeking the depth of relationship a group will never be able to provide. There is often a tragic underlying sense of loneliness about these people—the loneliness of being generalized, of being accepted as a person just because one is a person, rather than being valued for one's special qualities as a *specific* person. There is no substitute for the kind of relationship in which two people experience each other in all of their depths, knowing each other as they uniquely are. In fact, it is only in such encounters of depth that the most essential parts of our humanness can emerge.

IMMATURE BEGINNINGS

In counseling I have discovered that troubled marriages are often begun on a basis other than a depth of love, understanding, and commitment. No matter what the age of the partners, many people seem to begin marriages immaturely and to continue them in the same way. One or both of the partners may have sought marriage as a way of demonstrating adulthood, attractiveness, or virility/femininity. Marriage may have been sought as a substitute for the lost security of one's childhood family or as a sign of independence from it. One may want to "win the hand" of someone as proof of his or her power to conquer, persuade, or seduce. Marriage can even be the result of the lingering social pressures to keep sex and living together within the confines of a legal relationship. It can be a cover-up for pregnancy or, more likely, a way of giving legality and some sense of security to a child to be born. One couple who came to me even said that they wanted to be legally married so they wouldn't have any more hassles with landlords who did not want "loose livers" in their buildings.

For young people there is also the pull of romance. Teenage love has been the subject of romantic literature at least since the time of *Romeo and Juliet*. It is nice to feel in love, to be playfully in love, and to cherish the feeling so much that you want to express its importance and your happiness about it in a wedding. Weddings themselves are loaded with romantic symbolism. The problem is that romantic love can be superficial. Loving is not just something felt. It is a *process* of relating —ever-growing, changing, deepening, and discovering. It is much more than the playfulness and the delight that come with the romance of a courtship. I have experienced such romance twice in my life. It has felt great. In fact, nothing else can feel quite like it. But that feeling alone is not enough to base a marriage on. There has to be more than romance to a relationship if it is to be able to sustain itself when the romantic period is over—and, like it or not, the first flush of romance always runs its course.

Another immature sort of entrance into marriage— *pre*mature might be a better word for it: pre-knowing of oneself—is choosing a spouse as a substitute for a valued family member. In his book *The Death of the Family*, David Cooper points out how common, and how dangerous, are such marriages. He says that the family model of relationships is unhealthy because it encourages people to "glue" themselves onto others, just as a mother who feels incomplete without her child may hold the child to her instead of helping the child to move out into the world on his or her own.

A family model of roles and dependencies can stifle a couple's ability to define for themselves their own style of relationship. In the family model there tend to be all sorts of rules and rituals of behavior which, like some schooling, replace the creativity and inventiveness of free interchange with mechanical game-playing. The family model also is loaded with elaborate taboos which are enforced through the mechanism of guilt, taboos often relating to such things as ways of touching and, most importantly, to tenderness. According to Cooper, tenderness is a primary casualty in relationships based on the family model. He believes that the only way a person can achieve a deep and lasting relationship with someone else is to go through a kind of emotional divorce from one's parents and siblings. Without this separation all the things wrong in our older marriage and family models are going to be perpetuated into the future—and people made miserable in the process.

Intuitively, most people seem to know this. They seem to realize that the fullness and depth of a relationship depends on those involved respecting and valuing the autonomy of the other. The only problem is that it is difficult to shuck off one's past and forget the models with which one has grown up. This is exactly what must be done by people desiring relationships in depth, however. The difficulty of doing it seems worthwhile. At least in my own case, life has been made much more meaningful because of the deep and loving one-to-one relationships I have been able to form in maturity, on a basis of freedom and autonomy.

CAN MARRIAGE WORK?

Several years ago I wrote a letter to my sister on the eve of her wedding. I wanted to share with her a reminder of the se-

riousness of the intention she shared with her husband-to-be.
I wanted to convey whatever perspective I had gained from
my own marriage of, then, ten years.

A lot has happened since then. My sister has settled into
what seems to be a happy suburban life with a fine husband
and beautiful child, while I, after a great deal of inner turmoil, testing, and thought, have gone through a separation
and divorce, into another marriage. Whatever perspective I
had wanted to share with my sister at the time of her wedding, it was not sufficient to keep together my own first marriage, though the woman with whom I shared that marriage is
a person whom I still value and respect. In spite of the goodness of the years we had shared, the time came to admit that
we would be better off apart than together.

Neither of us wanted this to happen. Separation and divorce are agonizing experiences, even under the best of circumstances. I, my former wife, and our children must live
with the feelings of guilt, resentment, regret, and sadness that
go with the breaking up of a family and the building of separate, even if interrelated, lives. But my former wife and I
began our marriage prematurely, before we really knew
ourselves—and the selves we later discovered did not match.
Though it was hard to do so, we came to accept this and to
understand that no amount of counseling or attempts at
achieving better communications could create for us what
wasn't there—the desire to live in a centered way with each
other.

Certainly, in the midst of my own difficulty with marriage,
I became skeptical about its general workability. I doubted
whether *any* two people could live together with the heavy
weight of responsibility modern marriage involves, especially
given the romantic expectations of it I have already described. The more I read about the development of family
structure and the institution of marriage, the more I wondered whether the depth of love and understanding I have
come to believe is essential to any meaningful relationship
could be realized within an institution such as marriage,

which had come to have so many other requirements.

The case seems to be, however, that the breakdown of the ideal of the picture-book marriage in our society has come not so much from economic, child-rearing, and other institutional demands as from a breakdown of the centered relationship people have come to expect to be at the heart of a marriage. In a society which places such a high value on love and romance, and which now tolerates alternatives to lifelong monogamy, it is not surprising that merely the functional responsibilities of marriage are no longer able to keep many families together. Those who value love and passion want to experience them in their relationships. Those who value the knowing kind of loving I have described want to be able to experience it. Missing these qualities in their marriages has driven many people to seek them in relationships with others. A marriage should not be brought into being in the first place unless a couple believes as deeply as they can that such qualities are and will continue to be present in their relationship with each other.

HOW COMPLICATED IT GETS

I once talked with a woman who, as she puts it, had "flunked out" in her first marriage and in several other relationships. Mona had been married twice, the first time when she was eighteen. She was the second in her crowd to be married, and she remembers how special she felt. She and Roger, her husband, were almost smug in their self-confidence. They liked the attention they got from their friends, including all the questions about what it was like to be married. They had something the others didn't have. They also were paid a new respect and kind of attention from their parents. They were able to rejoin their families as adults, just as had their older brothers and sisters after they had been married. Of course they were still more dependent on their parents than they would have liked to admit. They had not really gotten settled in life nor developed careers for themselves. But it felt right to get married and to have all the rights and privileges that went with it. There was a lot of love, too. Just as soon as they could, they wanted to have a baby. Mona had trouble conceiving, but eventually a baby came—and then another and another. The romance didn't last, though. The babies radically changed Mona's life while Roger's attempts to find enjoyable work traumatized him. It took a long time for Roger to find himself, and as he did, he found himself less and less interested in Mona. To put it briefly, after eight years Mona and Roger hated each other more than they loved each other; and their hatred killed whatever mutual respect they had. It took them another two years to come to grips with this and be divorced.

Mona liked neither herself nor any of her "lovers" in the many relationships that followed. It took her seven years to realize this and do something about it. Finally, after therapy and a good and affirming friendship with another woman, she was able to detach herself from the past, to understand her premature reasons for wanting to be married to Roger, and to accept all the good and the bad of their marriage as past history to be learned from. Feeling free, she met Mike. As she put it, "Going to bed together is fantastic. I never knew before what it meant to make love with someone, though I bet I've done everything it's possible to do. I even did it upside down with a guy once. God, that was a weird thing to do! With Mike it's different. We make love all the time, with our eyes, with our voices, in how we make breakfast together in the morning. And it's infectious. Sure we fight. We do all sorts of things that go wrong. But we talk about it. I want to talk about it, and so does he. I've never shared things that matter to me with anyone like I do with Mike. It's like being naked all the time—and liking it. My whole body breathes now. I used to choke a lot. My kids, our friends, they all seem to feel what's going on. They tell me I look happy. I feel like it! I don't know what I expect will come of all of this, but I'm no dummy any longer. For the first time I want, and thoroughly like being with, someone else and can't imagine it being any different tomorrow." It was my delight to help Mona, Mike, her children, and their friends celebrate the beautiful centeredness that had grown between them.

Mona's former husband came to the same realization through another route. Roger had remarried soon after his divorce. Sharon, his new wife, was attentive and caring. Living with her was a real relief after all the hostility with Mona, but something was missing. Roger didn't feel any passion, any real enthusiasm, in being with Sharon. Then along came the book *Open Marriage*. Roger was intrigued with the idea of open companionship—with the idea of opening up a marriage so that it could include other relationships—but he missed what the O'Neills were saying. The O'Neills made it clear in their book that while opening up to other relationships and working at eliminating jealousy can enhance a couple's life together, unless that couple is secure in its own relationship, this opening is more likely to have the opposite effect. Sharon tried to be tolerant of Roger's other relationships, but it became clear that whatever passion and enthusiasm he showed others was not being offered to her.

Sharon was never thoughtful enough about her relationship with Roger. When the idea of open marriage came along she accepted Roger's arguments as reasonable, without testing out her own feelings. It made sense to her, at least intellectually, when he explained to her that jealousy was a "learned" emotion and that a "mature" person should be free of it and able to tolerate a spouse's intimate relationships with others. She thought that maybe he was right—that he would be happier if he could relate to other women; perhaps that would give some new life to their marriage. But what she discovered was that it didn't work that way either for him or for her. Instead of feeling better, she found herself feeling insecure, unhappy, resentful, and guilty. She hadn't turned out to be the perfect kind of wife she had hoped to be.

In case after case of experimenting with outside relationships, what appears to happen is that one partner ends up trying to manipulate the other into acceptance of a particular form of behavior with little or no concern for the other's feelings or values. There is no way for this to be of benefit to a relationship. Instead, it is more likely to trap the partners into an escalating cycle of experimentation and resentment in which there is less commitment, less communication, and less satisfaction within their relationship. If this escalation isn't checked, they are bound to lose the love and respect necessary for maintaining a worthwhile relationship.

OPEN RELATIONSHIPS AND COMMITMENT

After the publication of *Open Marriage*, my colleague Bill Houff wrote an article in *The Journal of Liberal Ministry* in which he reflected on his experience in counseling people who had decided to experiment with the idea of open companionship. He concluded that few of the people had begun their experimenting with an accurate conception of the strengths and weaknesses of their own marriage. They "thought" they could handle more than they could and that things would be the same after they came home from their dates. They also thought they could tolerate their spouses' attention to others. Seldom did things work out so well.

This is an important warning. It is important to be sure of our motives, to be in touch with ourselves, and to be knowing, valuing, and secure in our centered relationships, before relating outward. As I've stated before, most of us want and need relationships of a meaningful sort with people other than our partners. Such interactions are important to our personal fulfillment. But we must also know the risks that opening up can entail.

Intimate relationships create feelings of responsibility. I know that I have never been intimately involved with someone and been able to walk away from the relationship without being deeply affected by it. Because of this sort of realization, most people limit the extent to which they will become involved with others. Without such limitations, the risk of damage to the relationship that matters most—the relationship with one's partner—is too great. As people, we have taken and will continue to take a lot of risks in interaction with others, but the moment it begins to feel as though these outside relationships are encroaching upon our centered relationship, we should be prepared to pull back and reassess what's happening. *We've* got to check out what's happening, for if we *both* don't do this, something's changed about the openness, the honesty—the knowing—of our own relationship.

When I was trying to sort out my feelings and thoughts about marriage and open relationships I discovered Carl Rogers' book, *Becoming Partners*. Reflecting on his long career in counseling, Rogers concluded that the tugs and pressures on his own marriage were no different from any other. What made his marriage work, however—the thing he found that made marriage in general work—was that it was not tied to a certain model; his marriage was flexible. Rogers had talked with couples who had created good marriages in a wide variety of ways. What had made these partnerships rich and fulfilling was the sense of dedication each of the partners felt toward making as much as they could not only of their individual and mutual lives, but of the *relationship* too. They were not neutral toward their marriages. The relationships themselves were seen as important to individual fulfillment. Because the couples believed this, they were able to make knowing commitments to a constant process of changing and reshaping their relationship in whatever ways were necessary to the vital forces in their own growth and love.

For all that has been written about what makes a relationship work, nothing is more important than such an ongoing commitment. Without intending to maintain such a commitment, without deeply feeling a desire to do so, no one should enter into marriage, no matter how romantic it might seem. Living a life very different from that of Hannah and Paul Tillich, Helen and Carl Rogers never believed that feelings of love and romance would be enough to sustain their marriage. They had to continually affirm their choice to live and grow *together*, and to value their relationship as important in itself.

Through risking open communication, by accepting work-able roles in shared life, and by moving beyond such roles to an enhancing discovery of themselves and each other within their marriage, they managed to do this. They encountered the same temptation, made the same mistakes, and suffered the same pains as other couples, yet the Rogerses managed to find what he calls "growthful" solutions to whatever problems arose.

A marital relationship must be based on more than romantic feelings. It must include a *decision* to do everything necessary to sustain the relationship, a decision which must be reaffirmed over and over again. This is not an easy thing to do, and it does not always work, but a marriage or any other kind of close relationship stands little chance of enduring in a lasting or fulfilling way unless this decision is made.

In his book *the secret of staying in love*, John Powell, a Jesuit colleague, says that to be happy in their love, people must want to achieve a fullness of sharing with their partners. This sometimes requires doing things that are painful—being honest when we'd rather not be, talking when it would feel better to pout, admitting to our own embarrassing feelings when we would rather cast blame on someone else, staying when we would rather run away, admitting uncertainty rather than pretending to be certain, and speaking the truth as we see it rather than letting things pass without comment. None of these things is liable to bring peace and immediate joy to a relationship. They may, in fact, create pain and dis-comfort. But they make a relationship real, and they bring to it the possibility of a richness impossible without risking in such ways.

Being committed to making use of the possibilities of a marriage must be coupled with *responsible caring*. For any marriage to work there must be an investment by each of the partners in the well-being of the other, coupled with a self-valuing and a self-respecting without which neither would have anything of worth to share. This ensures that there will be no game-playing or inauthentic behavior in a relationship, and that those involved can feel free and secure to be loving without having to demand being loved. They can fully and responsibly care for each other and trust that their marriage will endure.

For all of this to work, however, there must be *openness* in a couple's relationship. I do not mean the openness of an unrestricted sanction to turn from one's spouse and to become involved with whomever one desires. While I believe we all need to have more than just our centered relationship to fulfill ourselves as individuals, it is the openness of people to communicate the important things going on inside themselves and within their centered relationship that is crucial to its survival, not their openness to other relationships on the part of their spouses.

Most couples are far too closed in their sharing with each other. The Center for Policy Research in New York City released a study not long ago in which it was estimated that the average middle-class American couple spends only twenty-seven minutes a week in meaningful dialogue! If we are to be honest about the quality of most of our conversations this should not sound so surprising. But it is a damning comment on us if that is all the time we have to spare for meaningful sharing with those for whom we care.

The openness required in a good marriage is more than open communication, however. There must be, as well, an openness to letting the roles and responsibilities within the relationship flow from the needs, resources, and possibilities of the individuals involved, rather than from one's concepts of what one *should* be or do. Luckily, these days, the redefinitions being called for by the women's movement are beginning to free us all to be more humanly ourselves. Today's good marriages are those in which both husband and wife are as free to be themselves when they are together as when they are apart.

Good marriages, good relationships in general, also require *joyousness*. To be responsibly caring and open does not mean being somber. Good relationships must be more than hard work, though hard work they do require. There must be an "up" to them—a feeling good. We are entitled not only to feel good about ourselves, but to feel good about our relationships. If we do not feel good about them, we had better watch out. No matter how much we may want such relationships to succeed, magic will not make this happen. While there may be an element of mystery in why certain relationships work as well as they do, opting to be joyful is not all that mysterious. Like many of the other things discussed in this book, joyousness, too, involves a choice—the choice of both partners. In good relationships the people involved choose to celebrate themselves and their relationship—to *do* those things which will create happiness for both and to *avoid doing* those things which won't. The preciousness of a good relationship is more worth celebrating than almost anything else I can think of. Celebration enriches and reaffirms a relationship in a special and irreplaceable way, whether the celebration is an unexpected kiss or a shared reaffirmation of the meaning of a marriage on one of its important anniversaries.

A final element common to good marriage is *a sense of the long run*. Life must and should have immediate satisfactions, but if a person gives in too much to immediate impulses, he or she can hurt an unprepared partner and damage possibilities for their relationship in the future. Everything one does in a relationship should have a sense of timeliness about it and feel appropriate to do both for now and for the future. All too often people ignore the negative warnings inside themselves about what they want to do, rationalizing the feelings away. We have to be able to forgive our own and our partner's mistakes, shortcomings, and hurtings; but we must also learn how better to avoid inappropriate and damaging behavior before it results in something that needs to be forgiven. It is impossible to avoid making mistakes in a relationship. But we should never ignore the other's feelings or behave in ways in which we have not learned from our previous mistakes. If this happens often it will threaten the basis of trust on which good relationships must be based and will make forgiving less and less possible.

There are risks in living together, in making a commitment to try everything in one's power to sustain a relationship. No one will ever find all the satisfaction one needs in a single relationship, but there is no substitute for what a deep and knowing, centered, one-to-one relationship can mean. It is because of this, rather than for the protection of children or for economic reasons, that marriage remains a good option of a society so filled with alternatives.

6

Honesty and Anger

About the same time I encountered Ken Kesey and his Merry Pranksters, I discovered Lenny Bruce. I was impressed with Bruce. Though no longer as funny as he once was, he still was obsessed with honesty. I valued that, seeing him as a religious person, a man driven to be a prophet, speaking the truth no matter what the consequences. From him, and from his ability to cut through the superfluous (he would have used a more colorful expression), I came to appreciate how important the avoidance of dishonesty was for me.

BEING HONEST

Honesty is an elusive concept, though I have asserted that the health of a relationship depends on the honesty and openness of those involved. Openness is easier to understand: it means being receptive, not filtering out or blocking off whatever comes in; it means nondefensive listening and experiencing. Honesty is usually thought of as telling the truth, a la Lenny Bruce. But what truth is it we tell when we are being "honest"? "Honesty" can be used as easily to hurt and shove someone away as it can be used to help and encourage further dialogue. For this reason, the truth should always be conveyed caringly, with a concern for the one to whom it is addressed.

   Lenny Bruce sometimes forgot this. He often did not care what his audience thought. A couple wishing to maintain the health of their relationship cannot be so care-less. Whenever I say something "in honesty" to my wife I must check out my motives. If I am expressing a simple judgment about the value of something she is doing, that's one thing. She is free to accept or reject my view without either of us having to feel bad about it. I may see something she doesn't, or the reverse may prove to be true. If we are being open with each other and sharing in a context of trust, love, and respect, telling each other how we see things is helpful. It expands our perspectives. It gives us eyes and minds beyond our own. But if the "truth" we speak is really a put-down or an expression of blame, then we have other motives.

Blame is an attack. It is meant to hurt, not help. Psychodynamically, a person blames both because it feels good, increasing one's sense of self-esteem and righteousness, and because it is a way of relieving one's own guilt. According to Herbert Fingarette, who explores the subject in his book *The Self in Transformation*, blame is triggered from a feeling of "I'd do that, if I could," more than from a belief that the other person has done something wrong. Rather than feel guilty about oneself, the blamer projects the feeling onto the other person so the blamer can condemn it. The problem is that not only does this keep the blamer from dealing with his or her own feelings, but the blame may not fit its object. If it doesn't, the person blamed is likely to become upset and cast blame back. A cycle of hostility is then set in motion which may become difficult to check.

Though there are problems with being honest, they can be avoided if we are willing to be care-full in our honesty, truly caring about the other person and ourselves. It is as impor-tant to remember this when being honest with ourselves as it is with others. Being care-full, however, does not mean that we should deceive ourselves. Self-deception has to do with repressing things that may be true because believing them would spoil our self-image. An example of this is the mother who refuses to believe her son has stolen something, even when she is confronted with the evidence. To admit he has done so would be to admit that he is not the "good boy" she envisages. According to Hannah Tillich, Paul Tillich chose to deceive himself not only about his relationships with other women, but about hers with other men. He did not want to have to deal with the contradictions between his behavior and his often-written-about moral values. As we have seen, this sort of dishonesty prevents both the individual and the couple from coming to grips with important things going on between them, including behavior damaging to their relationship. It is easy for self-deception to get out of hand and go beyond damage to the complete destruction of the relationship itself. For all of these reasons, the avoidance of dishonesty in a marriage is important, though it is equally important that the truth never be spoken without care.

GETTING ANGRY

One of the reasons I like being a Protestant minister instead of a Roman Catholic priest is that Protestants don't provide their clergy with special protections, like celibacy or ecclesiastical authority. Protestant ministers not only have the privilege of living like other people, but we must admit to human feelings without any divine excuses. We laugh, cry, and get angry, just like everyone else.

This was not easy for me to admit at first. I didn't have any problems with laughing and crying. Happiness and sadness seem like normal-enough emotions. It is hard to imagine anyone, even a "person of God," who is never sad. It is tragic to think of someone never happy. But angry? If ever there was someone who was not supposed to lose his or her temper, to get upset with people, it was that advocate of love—the minister. The problem with this stereotype was that I confused anger with hatred and hostility. Hatred, rather than anger, is non-love. Anger is an expression of displeasure, often appropriate. Anger is not antithetical to love, and not an inappropriate emotion for a person who cares about people.

While I am still a bit uncomfortable with myself when I get

upset, not always being sure why I am upset, I no longer believe it is "bad" to be angry. The saints could get angry, the prophets were always angry (they wouldn't have been prophets if the weren't), and even Jesus could go into a rage when he encountered something as distasteful to him as the moneychangers in the temple. Thus anger is a normal human emotion that, if allowed to be freely and appropriately expressed, can *add* to our personal health and well-being.

The issue, then, is not whether or not it is all right to feel anger. There is no right or wrong to this feeling. Instead, the issue is what *becomes* of our anger when we let it loose. Do we express it in appropriate ways at the right times—times when the stimulus for the feeling originally occurs—or do we repress our angry feelings, trapping ourselves in our own rage and risking later outbreaks that are likely to be destructive and directed toward the wrong object? Bottled-up anger is a poisonous demon, bound to create havoc when it breaks loose.

BOTTLING UP

Of course, if our image of ourselves is that of a person who is always under control, none of this makes any difference. Being "cool" has its place. We all need to control our emotions and behavior within limits. Too many things are going on in our lives at the same time to be able to respond to them all at once. But we ought to be wary about how and how much we limit ourselves. If we try to be too "cool" we are going to bottle up unresolved feelings about which something will eventually have to be done.

Dr. Theodore Rubin's *The Angry Book* is one of the best books ever written on the subject of anger. In it he says that bottled-up anger creates a slush fund, a store of subconscious memories of displeasures and the repressed feelings that go with them. This slush fund acts like an emotional poison, affecting all sorts of other feelings and behavior and building up each time we think we have a better way of dealing with an angry feeling than by expressing it—as when, to paraphrase Rubin:

We put it down . . .	"Oh, I don't really care about that" or "Sure I'm angry, but I won't give in to it."
We put it off . . .	"I'll wait until I cool down before I say something."
We put it onto something else less threatening . . .	"I really should be angry at myself, and not him."
We dilute it. . . .	"It's not her fault. It's this damn world in which we live."
We freeze it . . .	"I'm really upset, and I guess I'll just stay that way."

With the use of such mechanisms, slush funds grow. They don't remain inactive—anger feeds on itself. Bottled-up slush funds turn into demons capable of breaking loose at any time in ways always destructive, often unpredictable. Repressed anger can take poisonous twists resulting in anxiety, depression, obsessions, compulsions, phobias, denial, and self-sabotage. It undermines self-esteem. It feeds paranoia and cynicism. It magnifies faults, isolates the angry person from others, and makes it more and more difficult for the angry one to relate to others in any sort of positive way. According to Rubin, symptoms of an anger-tied person can be over-sweetness, talking too much, over-interest in sex, overeating, or overdoing anything. They also might include pretending, bullying, manipulating, playing the savior, hitting and running, malicious truth telling, being a joker or a bore, or "stewing in one's own juices." All of these behaviors represent hurtful, counterproductive ways of living, very damaging to the relationships of those involved. All are symptoms we have seen in ourselves or others when feelings of anger have not been resolved.

Sometimes slush-fund poisoning results in chronic twisted

behavior. Other times it results in explosions: violent out-breaks of destructiveness directed against oneself or others. Rubin says this is the price we pay for allowing anger to accumulate. Acts of destructiveness are bound to happen when we fail to deal with our feelings of displeasure *when* they occur. What results are eventually unbridgeable gaps between people and the sources of their anger.

OUT OF THE MORASS

The way out of the morass of repressed anger and its effects is to analyze it. The first step in doing this is to accept anger as a normal and reasonable emotion; it expresses displeasure. Anger is healthy as long as its expression is a warm and alive feeling directed toward its source. If this happens then a give and take can follow in which valuable emotional information can be exchanged. As a result, things can be done to relieve the anger, even if it's only to damn the circumstances that caused it. Such expressions are usually self-limiting. Feelings are expressed and there is a response—something happens and it's all over. Then the anger can fade away. This is especially true when the feelings are expressed as soon as they are sensed. Not only does this clear out the feelings, it gives the other person a chance to understand what's going on. Otherwise, he or she cannot be sure how we feel.

About a year ago, there had been a long weekend of special events in our church. I was worn out from working on them. The building was constantly filled with outsiders who had little concern about the church or what it represented. After the concert that climaxed the weekend's events I found myself nearly alone at four in the morning having to clean up a huge mess in preparation for the Sunday service. A couple was sitting in the middle of the clutter, and I asked them to go, but they wouldn't. My sleeplessness and frustration, my anger at being left to clean up—and allowing myself to be put into this situation—became too much when added to the insolence of the couple. I got so angry I blew up at them. As soon as I had exploded I knew I had made a mistake. The couple was only a small part of why I was angry. My only saving grace was that I didn't run; I hung in and, with the patient understanding of my wife and others to whom I turned, I was able to let the anger run its course. Gradually, I sorted out the sources of the anger and, one by one, resolved them, including explaining to the couple why my feelings were so strong. I told them I was sorry for what I had done, and I was. But I was not sorry I had gotten angry. The sources of my anger were all things about which I was legitimately displeased. The couple on whom I had vented my anger understood this, so they were willing to forgive what I did, if not forget. I was able to do the same for myself.

Because of experiences like the one I have just described, as well as reading people like Rubin, I've come to believe that the only kind of situation in which it's inappropriate to express anger is the one in which we don't understand the source of our anger. When we get upset we must stop and ask ourselves why we are feeling the way we do—and take the time to find the answer. If answers don't come and we are unable to help each other, then it's time to turn to those trained to provide therapeutic aid to help us get in touch with the roots of our feelings.

Clearing out bottled-up anger and the hostility and hatred that come from it isn't easy. It requires a great deal of effort. In a relationship it also requires the patient understanding and perseverance of the nonangry partner. With insight and effort an angry person can pull himself or herself back together and learn how to deal more immediately and directly with feelings. It is only when we can do this, when we can hold our demons in proper perspective, that we can keep them from getting out of hand and destroying the very things about which we care—like the love we share with someone else. As Paul put it in his Letter to the Ephesians:

Therefore, putting away falsehood, let everyone speak the truth with his neighbor, for we are intimately related to one another. Be angry, but do not sin: do not let the sun go down on your anger, do not give the devil that sort of foothold.

7

Love, Sex, Caring, and Being Friends

A few summers ago I attended a Sexual Attitude Reassessment (S.A.R.) seminar being offered to professionals by The Center for the Program in Human Sexuality at the University of Minnesota. While most of what was presented in the S.A.R. was familiar to me, the experience had its intended effect: I had affirmed once again that it isn't the sort of sexual contact people have with each other (or the lack of it) that matters—it's the quality of their relationships. To be fulfilling, sex must find its appropriate place within a relationship, and not the other way around. For this reason, licensing of sexual contact has never made sense to me. The sexual part of a relationship must evolve in its own way and in its own time, and must be flexible enough to grow and change, as a couple grows and changes.

Recently, when the wife of the former President of the United States revealed her views on premarital sex, her comments upset a lot of people. It seems to me that Betty Ford was quite wise in saying that her concern as a parent was not whether her children refrained from sex before marriage, but whether what happened in their relationships grew out of love, caring, and respect for themselves and those with whom they were involved. Legal documents cannot provide the love and respect necessary for a good relationship. We all know that. We also know, even if we don't always show it, that without these same qualities sexual relating is bound to become empty and mechanical. There's no joy in a pornographic film, even if the people in it are married. If the sexual relating in a marriage is like that of a pornographic film, the couple had better watch out. It is likely that love and respect are missing from their relationship.

This was the implication of what I heard Betty Ford saying, and it was also the message of the opening day of the S.A.R. Imagine being in a dimly lit room, the floor of which is covered by a sea of paisley-patterned pillows. Now visualize an attractive, smiling couple speaking in front of a room-length screen on which is projected a beautiful Minnesota landscape. Everything is being done to make us feel at ease as the couple leads us through films and discussions of the varieties of human sexuality. The films presented are positive, affirming, and in the best of taste. The experience becomes a kind of mellow, erotic high. Then comes dinner, the breaking up into small groups for further in-depth discussion, and a return to the room of pillows. "The Evening Film Festival" follows. A montage of sounds and images spreads out across the walls with dozens of films of animals and people engaged in an almost unbelievable and unending variety of sexual encounters. Organs move in and out of each other. It is almost too much to handle: overkill. By the end of one hour it would have been pure torture to have to sit through one more film. It was impossible not to be aware of the difference between the beauty of the sexual relating in the context of love, care, and respect—the context of intimacy—seen earlier in the day, and the ugliness of the pornography.

INTIMACY

Ronald Mazur's *Commonsense Sex* is an excellent study of the relationship between intimacy and physical sex; I think it's the best book ever written about sexual ethics. According to Mazur, the problem we face in a relationship is never "to bed or not to bed"; it is "to become or not to become" in a way in which the personhood of *all* involved is enhanced. He writes:

. . . one can become a better or more whole person through responsible risks in interpersonal encounter. The religious issue is thus one of chastity. "Are my motives, intentions, and sensitivity to the other as pure as can reasonably be expected . . . ?"

Today, chastity means acting with integrity. The point is that either a virgin or a nonvirgin ought to be chaste—this is the essence of the single standard of sexual behavior. This quality makes a difference in how we look at ourselves. It provides us with the strength of self-respect which enables us to learn from, rather than be crushed by, whatever unanticipated painful experiences we may have, so that if the path of "going all the way" is chosen, we will not end in a dark pit of remorse, but will discover a highlight in the fascinating journey of becoming.

Thus the key to the meaningfulness and satisfaction of relationships is not whether or not *sex* is present; it is whether or not *intimacy* is. The kind of intimacy which is a key to a loving relationship involves a process of sharing with another person in which it is possible for those involved to become more, rather than less, than they were before. To be lovingly intimate with someone we must want to accept the other as he or she is. We must honestly respect and value the other as a person of integrity and worth, as well as being someone with whom we desire to be. To be intimate, people must be willing to be exposed to each other in the full nakedness of their beings, to be "known," as I have put it before. They must want to relate as "Thous," in the most personal and full way possible.

For me, and I think for Betty Ford too, the only thing wrong about relating sexually or living together, in or out of marriage, is removing this relationship from the context of intimacy. To be both moral and happy in our relationships does not mean slavishly following the narrowly circumscribed do's and don't's of conventional morality. But it does not mean giving in to shallow romanticism or impersonal sex, either. If we can respect and care for the people with whom we choose to develop loving relationships, sex and/or whatever other forms of intimacy in which it becomes appropriate to share will find their place within our lives. There is no mystery to interpersonal ethics. We know when we are hurting or exploiting someone else, or being hurt or exploited ourselves. We also know (or soon learn) that negative behavior eventually becomes as destructive and self-defeating to us as it is to others. Balancing this is the fact that we also know how good it feels to enrich and be enriched by an intimate and growing relationship with someone else—to experience what it is that deserves to be called love.

LOVE

Love is probably the most misused of all the words in the English language. Still, it is hard to conceive of there ever being a healthy marital relationship without it.

Love happens; it cannot be forced, no matter how much it is longed for. As the great Jewish theologian Martin Buber puts it, the moments when love breaks through happen mysteriously, "shattering security." Marriage involves a decision. It is the choice of two people *in love*, to maintain a continuing relationship in which there is support, mutual growth, understanding, and respect.

Risking love involves tremendous responsibility. To love we must be not only willing to reveal our innermost selves to others, but willing to accept others as they reveal their innermost selves to us. Unfortunately, some people are reluctant to be open with others, and they discourage others from being open with them. They seem to fear the burden of responsibility that goes with being concerned about someone else. They also may fear that if they open up they will be hurt—that whatever they reveal will be misused by whomever they reveal it to. In either case they fear involvement, and they withdraw into themselves. The problem with this is that the memory and pain of non-love is worse than whatever discomfort might come from the failure of a love risked. Hell lies in a world of non-love we create for ourselves.

It is out of an awareness of this, I suspect, that most people are pushed toward love, even when they fear the possible results. Perhaps this is why the God who is love is portrayed in the Old Testament as a burning bush—with all the warmth and attraction, yet potential danger, of a fire.

We do risk danger in attempting to love. A façade of love can be used to control, hurt, or dehumanize. One psychologist, Lawrence Casler, says our society's emphasis on love is both the cause and effect of the insecurity, dependency, and conformity that may yet be the death of us all. According to Casler, saying we love someone is often just an excuse for manipulating them. Certainly the word *is* misused. My first counseling experience in the ministry involved an unwanted pregnancy resulting from a situation in which a man had said "love," meaning "I'd like to go to bed with you," and a woman had interpreted it as a promise of continuing affection and attachment.

Shulamith Firestone, one of the most challenging of all feminist authors, claims that love, even more than childbearing, serves as the "pivot" of women's oppression. This is so, she believes, because it is seldom a mutual experience. Rather, the concept of love is used to justify the feeding of men on the emotional strength of women. Those who are overly romantic about the notion of love owe it to themselves to read Firestone's book, *The Dialectic of Sex*. Only when there is a full and reciprocal mutuality of feeling, she asserts, can a healthy love exist.

Unfortunately, attempts at loving seldom are mutual. Returning to an earlier theme, the unequal balance of power between men and women is probably to blame for this. "Wham, bam, thank you ma'am," is still too often the goal of men in their relationship with women. Many women, feeling dependent on men for both emotional and economic support, feel they cannot afford the luxury of being spontaneous or selective in their loving. The love and approval of men is too important to them. So, as Simone de Beauvoir says in *The Second Sex*, both men and women become trapped in a game of sham love which is, in the end, satisfying to neither.

The analyses of feminists, such as these, cut deep. They cut as deep as the all-to-real sexism of our society. Yet their blame of men is too sweeping. Men, as well as women, seek the satisfaction and joy found in intimate relationships. The entrapments possible in love and sex and marriage are as destructive and confusing to men as to women. Because she is so skeptical of the ability of men to share equitably with women, Firestone seems to prefer the development of a society in which love, attachment, and even sex—at least between men and women—are shorn of their meaning and cast aside. I doubt, however, if this is the sort of world in which most of us would want to live.

I think there is wisdom in the ancient idea that rather than woman's being born of man, the original human creature was male and female together, a wholeness, until God came along and cleaved it in two. Ever since, these two parts of humanity—male and female—have sought reunion with each other. Whereas Firestone is absolutely correct in seeing sexual relating as more often a quest for conquest than for union, love, if it is truly love, is always an expression of a desire for unity—a desire to create a wholeness with another. But it is also more. Those who have truly loved have left the experience with something more than when they entered. This is why it is worth risking the dangers of the burning bush—why it is worthwhile to be open to love, even if the risks of its failure are great. When love is shared with a reciprocal mutuality it is not a destroyer but an enricher. The experiences we have of love, even if the loving fades, remain part of us and add to our wholeness for the rest of our lives. An experience of love, no matter how brief, always leaves one more of a person. Even Shulamith Firestone concedes this.

Love may or may not come often—and it may not last long when it does—but this does not make it any less desirable, nor any less important, as the basis of a committed relationship such as marriage. We should be open to it. Being an adult lover is not asking to be loved; it is being open to love and, as e.e. cummings puts it, being of love "a little more careful" than of anything.

As Bob Kimball, the Unitarian theologian, says, "Getting away with love isn't easy." We should not expect love to be easy, or unfrightening, or certain. Love involves risk. If there is no risk there is no possibility—and if there is no possibility, there is no growth. Like being twice-born, we must give of our lives—we must risk, if we are to find love. There is no intimacy without suffering and no guarantee of a happy ending in anything we do. The odds of life may weigh against the happening of love, but if we are not open to love we shall probably miss that sense of unity and wholeness without which we can never be complete.

LOVE, LIFE, AND DEATH

It took me a long time to process the experience of that first day at the S.A.R., but an idea expressed by one seminar leader proved to be very helpful. In talking about the meaning of sexual expression in his own life, he said it helped him to remember that human feelings are really evolutionary newcomers. In fact, all of the experiences that accompany our deepest feelings are relative newcomers to the cosmic order.

In the beginning stages of evolution there was neither sex nor death, nor any feelings about them. One-celled creatures divided and split, divided and split, on and on in an unbroken chain. Though they were unaware of it because they had no consciousness, these organisms were immortal. Remnants of their splitting cells probably still exist, and are still splitting. Somewhere along the chain of evolution, though, to enable life to cope better with new and more complicated circumstances (or, perhaps, just by chance), some of these single-celled organisms began to colonize, taking on more specialized tasks and functioning as more complex multi-celled organisms. Because simple cell division was no longer an adequate means of reproduction for these organisms, one solution that evolved was differentiation into separate sexes, each of which provided partial cells that then could be joined to produce completely new cells. These cells would then split and provide the differentiated cells necessary to produce an offspring of the parents. To accomplish all of this, sexual relations became necessary.

As evolution progressed, consciousness began to emerge in its higher forms. Along with the development of consciousness in human beings came feelings about sex and relationships—such as love—and feelings about death—such as fear. To be born as a distinct creature also meant to have to die—and to be human meant to be aware of both birth and death. Parents had to make space for their offsprings. So the cells of complex organisms eventually had to atrophy and die. Love, the joyous feeling which draws people together, then, is inexorably linked to death and all the foreboding that goes with it.

While we may wish death did not have to be a part of life's bargain, it is. While we might also wish we didn't have to be aware of the approach of death, without this awareness we would not be able to feel love. If to be able to love is to have to die, so be it. The joy of the one, it seems to me, is worth whatever fear we may have of the other. Love and life and death are inexorably mixed.

I don't want to sound too romantic about all of this. While it is true that love often does "just happen" and depends in part on forces over which we may have little initial control, the experience of love also depends on choices we make, and on circumstances in which it is possible. It *is* possible to be unlucky in love.

It is also possible to be confused about love. The word *love* is used for too many things—concern, friendship, attraction, affection. When I want to reach out to someone out of pure human concern, a better word to use than love is *agape*. Such caring is different from the desiring of erotic attraction, which is also sometimes called *love*. The Greek word for this is *eros*. Such caring is also different from brotherly or sisterly attachment, the Greek word for which is *philia*. The love about which I am talking is love in its fullness: a seeking of unity, depth, and fulfillment with another human being.

CARING

If this feeling of love is to be sustained with someone, there must also be caring. Caring is an active, outreaching verb, which comes from the root *caru*, meaning sorrow. *Caru* is akin to *kara*, meaning good, such as used in *Karfreitag*, the Gothic term for Good Friday—a day memorializing perhaps the supreme act of caring in the history of humankind. As a verb, caring means worrying about or feeling concern for. To be caring, we must be involved with and attentive to someone else—attentive in ways which are helpful to the other in his or her own becoming.

One of the models for caring in the New Testament, one I've often thought about when trying to discover what it means to care about others, is the story of the Good Samaritan. The story of the Samaritan is often misunderstood as an example of how we should "do good" by giving to those less fortunate than we. "Doing good" is not what the parable is about—we are being asked to care. The man lying by the road had a problem: he was hurt and could not get up. The Samaritan had resources: he had time to spare from his journey; he knew of an inn nearby; and he had enough money to provide the man with a room, a bed, and some food. Because he cared about life the Samaritan could not bear seeing a part of life wasted, especially when he could do something about it. He used what resources he had to provide the stranger with an opportunity to escape his suffering. Having given the man a chance to begin his healing, the Samaritan left him, knowing that it was then up to the man himself to use the resources he had been given.

The Samaritan was soft hearted, as a friend of mine, John Corrado, has put it, but hard headed. He realized both what he could do constructively for someone else and what his limitation was once it had been done. Having cared, he moved on, wondering, perhaps, what the stranger did with his chance, but not feeling bad or guilty at being unable to do more. The Samaritan did what he could—he paid attention. That is what matters.

Such caring is difficult. The men in the story were strangers; they had no personal feelings about each other. But caring seems no less difficult for two people who are intimately involved. In trying to care we can make mistakes, and we may hurt when we want to help. To help may even require hurting, which seems like a lousy bargain. What must count, then, is our intention. As long as we are trying to care, our mistakes are forgivable. What's wrong is to be afraid to care because what we do may go wrong.

My friend's suggestion that caring should always be "hard headed and soft hearted" sets the best criteria I know for being responsive to those we love. What this requires is working toward realistic understandings about ourselves, others, and the situations in which we find ourselves in a committed relationship, like marriage. This means being careful not to become either hard hearted or soft headed—an unfeeling or thoughtless person. It means recognizing and being honest with our feelings. It means unraveling what our relationships do and ought to mean for us. It means ferreting out and destroying the strawmen in our relationships that we may have set up to deceive ourselves or to avoid the discomfort of having to make decisions requiring a change in our behavior. It means summoning up the courage to confront and live with whatever pain may come from risking to care.

Whatever the changes that may be required, whatever the discomfort that may go with them, caring opens us to a better future—a future freed from whatever burden it was that required the risking of care in the first place. As in the case of the Samaritan, what's required is that we do what we can, rather than pass by. The pain of the guilt of passing by is a far greater burden than taking on whatever discomfort may come from caring. To be whole in ourselves we must be care-full, full of care for those whom we love—in fact, even for strangers.

To care is to show our love for others. To show our love for others is to express our love of life. It is the way to make *real* love in a marriage.

Having said this about love and caring, something needs to be said about friendship, another necessary though often ignored ingredient of a committed relationship. Lovers who are not friends make poor spouses.

"Oh, sure. I know her. She's *my friend*"—we use this phrase for many reasons. It is a way of saying that not only do we know the person, but the person knows us, i.e., we are significant enough to be known. We thus are able to share in whatever esteem is possessed by the person with whom we claim friendship. Claiming friends convinces us that we're important enough to be known, which, in turn, helps us feel that we are worth knowing, even when we may not be so sure this is true. But when we use the word "friend" in such a way we shouldn't deceive ourselves into thinking that we are talking about "friendship." Friendship is something very different, especially the friendship important to a marriage.

Friendship means more than recognition; it means more than liking or being liked. True friendship must involve acceptance, trust, and a sharing in depth with another person—a quality of intimacy and of love. It involves that special kind of loving in which there is a growing awareness of the uniqueness and value of one another, an affirming of the best in each other, and a mutual enrichment of the selves involved. It is a quality of relationship recognized as important to full personhood by all of the world's great religions. Guatama asked his disciples to postpone nirvana until they could help others achieve Buddhahood. Jesus asked his followers to "love thy neighbor as thyself." But it shouldn't take the authority of scripture to convince us of our need for friends. In their personal quest for meaningful and fulfilling lives, most people discover how important friendship is.

In *The Art of Loving*, Erich Fromm calls the love involved in friendship the fundamental kind of love underlying all others. By this he means that love in friendship includes the sense of responsibility, the care and respect, the "knowing" of the other, and the wish to enhance his or her life that are essential to a committed relationship. It is also the kind of loving that brings with it a sense of solidarity or union with all the rest of humankind. In a very real sense it is only in our capacity to love someone in a special way that we learn *how* to love others, and come to want to share our love with others. I remember a couple stating this beautifully in a wedding ceremony and then symbolizing it by sharing bread they had baked with the friends they had asked to be with them. They then handed out flowers to everyone and asked the whole gang to join them in a dance through the park and to give flowers to all the people they met. I felt love in a way that day I had never felt before. It made me want to love in return.˙ *

The caring central to the love in friendship takes effort; it doesn't come as easily as sharing flowers. Being a friend means paying attention in the fullest possible way. It means intensely *being* with the other. It also requires *patience*, a quality that is often ignored in our time-obsessed society. Finally, being a friend means *risking*, letting ourselves be known without being sure the other is going to like what's revealed. It means being open to being hurt, allowing ourselves to be vulnerable, as well as being affirmed. It means being willing to accept the other's openness and all that flows from it, becoming aware of his or her problems and being willing to respond even if it involves suffering or giving up something. The ability to love as a friend depends on being able to emerge from self-centeredness to shared centeredness with another. It requires having faith in the reliability and stability of friendships and the ability of people to care for and value each other. Such faith requires courage, for even with a lover one can never quite be sure of the response one will get. But without the risk, there is no growth. To grow we have got to take risks in love.

We *need* to love as friends—to care and be cared for. As

feeling, touching, conscious, social beings, eons beyond the cells from which we have evolved, we need intimacy and friendship. We need to be loved *and* loving. This means we must seek out relationships in which we can both geniunely be ourselves and grow with another. We need the kind of relationship Carl Rogers described his marriage as being.

The following letter I once wrote to a friend summarizes what I believe friendship to be. It is the same kind of letter I would write to my wife, if I were to describe the friendship we share.

Friendship can't be intellectualized; it's not something about which we can learn rules. Friendship and loving are arts, but not some kind of commercial art we learn so we can impress people. Friends are free individuals who risk being themselves with each other—people who share their uniqueness and delight in seeing each other grow as a result of their shared relationship. The minute they slip and the art becomes manipulation, like commercial art, friendship is gone.

To be friends, people must really *be* friends. The right things must happen when they are together—not enjoyment, although they do enjoy each other; not measurable growth, although they learn from each other and grow; not pleasant strokes, although they affirm and support each other—it's just that between them right things happen. The clues about the rightness—and about the love that goes with it—are in their eyes, in the tone of their voices, in their laughter, in the way they take leave of each other, in the warm feelings that linger on after they are apart. In place of a lusting or desiring there is a knowing that it is good when they are together—and that's enough. This doesn't sound very scientific, I know, but it *is* what friendship feels like.

Because what I am talking about is so important, I wish I had a magic formula for making friendship happen. I don't. We've got to take the risk of fumbling our way into friendships. We've got to be open to them and willing to reveal ourselves in them, with *all* that involves.

It's an "awesome responsibility" to have you as my friend. Never again can I not care what becomes of you or forget the feelings we now have for each other. It's an awesome responsibility, my friend, but it is one about which I feel good—one which helps me feel more complete, like more of a person than I would be without our friendship. I'm more because of our relationship. I hope the same is true for you. I'm glad we are friends.

Without friends, we cannot be fully human. We have to be, and to have, friends. Friendship is a risky business; it sometimes fails. But we have nothing to lose in trying to build friendships except our isolation and loneliness.

the
price
and joy
of
being
human
is
the possibility
of
feeling
good
while
tottering
on
the edge
of some
huge
possible
mistake
and
knowing
that
it
doesn't matter
whether
things
come out
o.k.

. . . that it doesn't matter, because we've got a friend. Friendship is the risk of living on the edge, but not alone.

8

The Question of Children

In one of the talks she gave this past year at the University of Cincinnati, Margaret Mead said that no matter how radically lifestyles may change, the one institution that will never disappear is the family. She claimed that no form, including the kibbutz, day care center, or whatever, has proven to be an adequate substitute for the loving presence of a mother and father in the rearing of children. She was not criticizing the day-care movement, or the idea that parents should not have to assume total responsibility for childrearing. If ever there was a person supportive of feminism and the freeing of men and women for full participation in society, it is Margaret Mead. Yet her personally and professionally informed point of view is that there is no substitute for the special kind of love and concern that a parent who has assumed specific responsibility for the well-being of a specific child can provide.

DECIDING

I have thought a lot about Dr. Mead's claim. Before we were married, Jan cared during the day for a beautiful little girl named Erin. Erin's mother is unmarried. The child's conception was completely unanticipated. But when her mother discovered she was pregnant, she was delighted. She had been married earlier and had tried without success to get pregnant. She had always wanted a baby, but thought it wasn't possible. Erin is well loved not only by her mother, but by the whole community of people to which her mother belongs.

Erin has been a lucky child. Some other children born outside of marriage are not so lucky. They must go without the nurturing and support of one of their parents. Often they must go without the nurture and support of either parent, as the parent left with the responsibility, usually the mother, finds herself unable to provide for the child's physical and emotional needs.

Even less lucky are children born to parents who discover they really don't want to be parents. A child has no choice about either being brought into the world or being brought into relationship with its parents. To decide to conceive a child, then, involves an unshirkable responsibility on the part of parents. No parent is ever free, morally, to walk away from his or her child—and no child should be conceived unless it can be born into a loving environment. In my own case, even though I ended my first marriage, there was no way for me to end my parenting—and I have never had a desire to do so. I am my children's father, with all that entails. It will never be otherwise. There is nothing voluntary about my relationship with my children. Frankly, I prefer it this way. Children have added a richness to my life every bit as important to me as the richness of marriage itself.

If partners are unsure of their desire to take on the burdens as well as the joys of having a child, they should not risk conception. Marriage begins as a relationship of choice between a man and a woman—and must have value for them whether they have have children or not. But children conceived by a couple are entitled to parents who will love them and provide them with a good environment in which to grow. I seriously question risking bringing a child into a relationship in which there is conflict, unsureness, or resentment about parenting.

RESPONSIBILITY

The responsibility about which I am talking is expressed in the Service of Dedication to Children, which, in my congregation, takes the place of the traditional baptism or christening of a child. In this service the parents, with their children, are asked to come forward both to celebrate the birth of their child and to reaffirm their commitment to it. The minister begins:

It is good, when new human lives have entered the world, for the children to be brought before the community of their families so that both the parents and the community, recognizing the importance of children whose thoughts and deeds will be creating the world of tomorrow, can dedicate themselves to play their part in the growth and creative nurture of the children. In this brief ceremony, we dedicate ourselves to supporting these newcomers to life and to help them walk in the ways of righteousness, truth, and love.

These children are only beginning to become the persons they will become. The process of their growth will often be difficult, so we must pledge ourselves to help them in it. The climate of love and understanding that surrounds them will help shape their lives. We must build a climate that will let them see as possible the development of wisdom, courage, kindness, and all else they will need to grow as persons. We must help them mature, at the same time that we allow them to hold on to as many of the qualities of childhood as they can while they grow up. Too many of us have given up the spontaneity and creative playfulness that is so much a part of being a child, for the sake of the deadly conventions and routines we associate with adulthood.

Having brought children into the world we must now love them, and we do. So it is, then, with both awe and joy, realizing the responsibilities and possibilities we have as the parents of these children and as the other adults of the community into which they have been born, that we welcome them into our midst and pledge ourselves to their nurture and support. We hope that, by making of our own lives all they can be, and by caring for these children in all the ways we can, their capacities for goodness and happiness will be realized. Our hope for them is that even if everything in their lives does not turn out all right, at least most things will be possible. You who are the parents of these children have the greatest responsibility of all.

Parents give to their children the bright knowingness of their eyes.
    Love you give them with your looks and lips.
From your smiles they will learn to smile in reply.

From your laughter will come theirs.
In response to your voices they will learn to make sounds,
   They will imitate your words and their minds take form.
From your walking they will learn to follow;
   From your gestures they will pattern their movements and inflec-
   tions.
Your goodness will become their good and your evil theirs,
   Or perhaps it will be the reverse.
The same for fears and doubts, wisdom, courage, openness, and joy.

Parenthood is a sacred and holy calling.

It is the highest of all dedications: dedication to the creation of a
human life and to help in the shaping of a child's mind, body, and
character. It stands above all the business and power of the world
as a parent's primary vocation, for it is certainly true, as the words
of religious tradition put it: What will it profit people if they gain
the influence and riches of things and fame and lose their children and their companionship? The wisdom of this is in recognizing not only what we have to give our children, but the richness
their lives bring to us. Understanding, then, the great responsibilities of parenthood, do you standing before us take upon
yourselves the privilege and responsibility of loving and caring
for these children in body, mind, and character, so that they
might be opened to rich, satisfying, and meaning-filled lives?

At this point, the parents respond and then the minister addresses the whole congregation:

These children are only beginning to explore and know the larger
world outside their homes. As they grow older they will live more
and more in this larger world and less and less in the shelter of
their parents. They will find that all is not love and protection in
the larger world. The world may frighten them with its confusion
and complexity, its ugliness and cruelty. At times life will be
lonely. But they will find beauty and love and joy and meaning
there, too, if they can be given support in being open to them.

We must do what we can to help these children become their
finest selves, to help them realize, as they grow, as many of their
potentials as possible. We must help them become persons worthy
of their humanity—persons dignifying in themselves and in their
actions the humanity of others.

The service then goes on to address the children, beginning with their naming:

> _____, we wish for you full and rich lives, lives in which you will work for the good of all through your thoughts, visions, and deeds. May you serve, with all of your mind and soul and strength, the ideals of truth and goodness—and may you find nobility of purpose in every day of your lives.

With a prayer, the service then comes to a close:

> We are grateful for new life, for the chance it gives us to better ourselves and for the rededication it inspires in each of us. Let the lives of these newcomers to our human family be filled with happiness and purpose and bring a freshness of promise to us all. Amen.

Jan and I were aware of the implications of parenting, spelled out in this service, when we decided that we wanted to share our relationship with a child. My former wife and I had a similar awareness when we made a similar choice. The feelings that have gone with these choices have been ones very much like the ones described in the dedication: "With both awe and joy, realizing *both* the responsibilities and possibilities." The possibilities that have followed because of what I have been able to share with my children have, indeed, been both joyful and awesome. My children have enriched my life in ways impossible without them. The responsibility side has been tougher.

PARENTING

Any couple, or any person at all, considering having a child must take seriously what this responsibility means. The oldest of my children are now teenagers. The issues of parenting in relation to them are much more complex than those in relation to the youngest child, who is still trying to figure out what it was he did that got him from his front to his back the other day. Matthew's ability to act on his own is rather limited at this point; the same is not true for my older children. Not only are they able to act on their own, they are acting in a world very different than the world of adolescence in which I "came of age."

When I was in the seventh grade, the major social event of the week was going to the movie on Saturday afternoon or getting asked to be a dance-mate by one of the more popular girls at dancing class. I am afraid that the days of white gloves and ice cream sodas for junior highers are now nothing more than nostalgia. Young people have joined in the cultural revolution that has gone on in our society—and anyone planning on having a child had better understand what this means.

Young people today are more worldly wise than their parents were when they were growing up. But being "worldly wise" does not always bring with it common sense, respect, or an attitude of caring. There remains a lot of child—a lot of inexperience, a lot of irresponsibility—even in an older young person. Sometimes the conflict between possibility and responsibility in their lives gets them and their parents into trouble.

Young people often do not recognize this conflict and their need to do so isn't helped by parents who, in their liberality, imply to their children that they don't care what the children do as long as the young people are willing to accept responsibility for what happens. This is a denial of the responsibility of parenthood. Pre-adults are usually physically, emotionally, and legally unprepared to accept full responsibility for their actions, and only partially aware of the implications of their behavior.

I am not a perfect parent—and my parenting is complicated by the fact that not all of my children live with me. But I take seriously the words of the dedication to children used in my church. I care about my children enough that I am not willing to be so "liberal" as to let their irresponsible behavior go by without trying to do something about it. I do not believe that any of my children has yet had enough experience or developed enough savvy to be able to gauge adequately the present and future effects of what they are doing. They are learning to do this, but learning takes time.

GROUND RULES

What I am saying may sound moralistic. I neither like moralists nor want to be moralistic. But problems like the availability of drugs to young people and a growing permissiveness about sexuality have forced me to think through what might be appropriate ground rules for those who are considering parenthood.

First, if we decide to have children, we should make our values clear to them as early as possible. We should let them know why we believe they should have to demonstrate an ability to handle problems before they earn the right to deal with them on their own. We should show them how we try to follow the guidelines we set for our own behavior. None of the rules we establish for our children should be rules we would not be willing to follow in the same circumstances. All too often, parents either set themselves above rules or are inconsistent in following them. Children know it when parents do this. There isn't much we can hide from our children.

Second, as parents we should provide children with appropriate ways to accumulate the experience they need to be able to make good decisions. Modeling behavior for them is one way. Doing this doesn't assume that our children will follow our example, but it will help. Presenting a balanced model of behavior in relation to alcohol, for instance, not only helps young people see how they might use that drug in an appropriate way, but it also may help them to avoid using other drugs in inappropriate ways. From watching parents children learn a lot about the kind of behavior which is good to emulate and that which is not. Unfortunately, many young people also learn how to misuse things (like drugs) from their parents.

Third, the adults who are around children should try to create, in the environment they share, a climate of acceptance and trust, so that the children will feel able to talk with them even after getting into trouble. Crises aren't bad. It is possible to build out of our responses to negative experiences an atmosphere of openness and trust in which young people will be able to share more and more of the important and confusing things upon which they need to reflect. Constructive parents are able to help their children see a wide variety of options available for growing into selfhood. Such parents make the environments that they share with their children places where all can be themselves and can enjoy being with each other.

Finally, parents and other adults who are around children can, as the saying goes, "get it together." Study after study shows that although young people are subject to tremendous peer and media pressures, they still tend to be either as healthy or as messed up as the adults with whom they relate. It's too much to expect our children to be "good" if we behave badly. Our children know us—they have a sense of how well or how badly we handle our lives. This means we are going to have to pay attention to our *own* behavior if we really care about how our children are going to behave.

One of the risks we take, if we decide to have children, is that they won't pay attention to us and will not respond to our concerns. Yet, if we are authentic and caring enough with them, realizing that sharing is not a one-way street, it is possible that they will ask us about things before making mistakes that will hurt both.

Life is a continual process of growing up. Every age has its own risks, problems, confusions, and pain. For people who lack enough wisdom or experience, the confrontations of life can become too much to handle. If we want to shield our children from life's confrontations while they are still under our care, it isn't because we want them to become dependent on us. It is because we don't want them so crippled that they can't function on their own. We hope they will feel an equal responsibility to shield us from their problems when we cannot handle them.

CHILDREN'S SEXUALITY

An area in which this is particularly difficult is that of sexuality. Though we have begun a program in sexuality for young

people and their parents in our church, few of the partici-
pants have felt comfortable discussing the subject. In an article that appeared a few years ago in the *New York Times
Magazine*, Anne Roiphe, who has written several pieces on
family life, said that the growing openness about sexuality
among high school and college people is creating problems
for their parents, especially parents who have younger children still living at home. I have had friends who found themselves in this position. They have wanted to be supportive and
understanding of their older children, but have been afraid
of what this might mean to younger siblings. I believe that
most of their fear actually comes from ambivalence about
their *own* sexual attitudes. There are very few married adults
who have not at least *wondered* what it would be like if they
could be sexually freer. When someone acting freer, especially a child, lets his or her behavior show, it comes too close
for many parents. It threatens to unlock their own carefully
maintained inhibitions.

A straightforward concern about the well-being of children
is also involved, however. Anne Roiphe asks herself how she
would feel if she were to find a container of Pills hidden
among the underwear of her daughter, who "still leaves rings
around the bathtub." Part of getting a handle on this, as I
have said before, is in realizing what the world of young
people is like today. Couples who come to me for weddings
are not ashamed of being intimately involved with each
other—and they shouldn't be ashamed. It's time that sex for
young people moved out of the backseat of cars into positive
and enhancing atmospheres.

I still believe my children can, and perhaps will, make serious mistakes in their relationships. They may allow themselves
to become physically involved with another and may feel bad
afterward. But that sort of thing happened in my own
growing-up days, as well. At least in the current environment
there is no pretense that boys just "sow their oats" with "other
kinds of girls," or that girls are satisfied with romantic novels
and horseback rides. The conversation in the girls' locker
room isn't much different from that in the boys' locker room.

On the other hand, the experience I have had in talking about human sexuality with young people suggests that boys are not different from girls in being most concerned about, and most confused by, the nonsexual side of intimate human relationships.

According to Roiphe, most of the memories that parents have of their children are of rites of passage: all the important "firsts." What goes into the scrapbook are pictures of the first steps, descriptions of the first words, records of the first bike rides without training wheels, the first report cards, and graduations. Jan and I already have for our scrap book a picture of Matthew with the odd look on his face after the first tumble over. For each of these firsts the parents can feel the pride that goes with knowing that they have helped their children cross over a threshold.

But the first words of whispered love, the first petting, the first Pill or condom, the first "going all the way," are things young people experience in private—and this is as it should be. The same is true for a lot of other firsts children have as they grow older, something difficult for many parents to accept, even though it is the way things have to be. What it tells them, whether the parents are aware of it consciously or not, is that they've served their parental function and their children are now at the point where they can live on their own. This means not only giving up their power over their children, but losing the status they have had because it was they alone who could do the "adult" things. At night it used to be the parents who had sex behind closed doors while their children wondered what was going on inside. Now it is the other way around. For even the most liberal parents, with the emerging openness about sexuality on the part of their children comes the groan: "Oh, no. Not yet!"

Of course, many of the fears of parents are legitimate. My own high school sophomore daughter looks a lot older than she is, and often behaves so. But there is still an adolescent inside her body, despite her appearance, and a lot of little girl in her. What she wants and needs is not all that clear. For many young people of both sexes, permissiveness about physical relationships is creating problems—from an increase in venereal disease and early pregnancy (made all the worse by the fear of adult condemnation), to the diminishing years of childhood allowed to young people. Much of the fault for this is ours. We want our children to grow up too early, to become like their Barbie or Ken dolls when they'd rather still be playing with teddy bears.

SHARING

Today's young people are faced with a whole range of new options and problems, among them the place of sexuality in their lives, which is hard not only for them to deal with, but for their parents to understand. One way parents can help children find their own way through this maze would be for parents to admit to their feelings, including their fears, and to share them openly with their children. It's wrong to ask either a parent or a child to sacrifice privacy, but each ought to be willing to speak in honest and direct ways with the other. Enough respect ought to be developed so that all feelings that need to be shared, including both happy and negative ones, can be shared.

Among the saddest things of life for a young person is to be afraid of sharing with a parent the happiness that comes with a breakthrough to intimacy. Often a parent is concerned about whether or not a teenager had sex the night before when the more appropriate concern should be about how happy and meaningful the teenager's life is and how well he or she is growing in ability to develop and nurture the kind of relationships that will be sustaining and fulfilling.

Parents open to sharing aren't all that young people need, however. It is also helpful for them to have other adults with whom they can share those things which matter most—and to have their parents realize that this is healthy and not a sign of disrespect or lack of love. We all need to talk about some things with people outside our primary relationships, whether we're young or not. This can be a tricky area, though. Young people don't always choose the right kind of people for their adult friends. Some adults make use of young people for their own ends—and both the young and their parents had better be aware of this. It is particularly dangerous when a relationship with another adult further alienates a young person from his or her own parents.

It's rough to be a parent today. It's rough to be a young person. The choices that have to be made are more confusing than ever. Parents would find it helpful if they could shoulder some of their fears and forget about the loss of the old status and authority they had with their children and begin to express their love and concern in new ways, as friends. The world in which we find ourselves is what it is, but so are the conditions available for fulfilling and meaningful lives, and relationships. With a little help, the cycle of the generations will progress in a healthy way and the young people coming to the ministers of the next generation to be wed will find as much happiness and purpose in their relationships as I hope the couples now choosing to wed, and perhaps bear children, are finding in theirs.

I am not sure how well I do as a parent, but I am trying to do my best to understand my children, and to be supportive of them as they try to make sense out of their lives and to make the right kind of choices. This includes letting them know what I think their proper limits ought to be, the kinds of questions they should be asking, and how I feel about what we both are doing. I am trying to learn how to laugh and cry and be openly overjoyed or torn up with my kids, as well as how to share my experience without demanding they follow my example. But, most of all, I am learning that what speaks loudest to my children is the model of my own behavior: the successes and failures of my own life. I can't fool them any more than I can fool myself. Coming to understand this was one of the healthiest things that has ever happened in my fumbling life. Standing naked with one's children is even riskier than standing naked with one's spouse. You may be able to walk away from the one, but never from the other.

9

Tensions in the Midst

Issues of childrearing and parenthood represent only one source of tension a couple may face as their marriage evolves. There are financial problems, conflicts over friends and interests, disputes over relatives, sexual tensions, and disjointed aspirations. The most disruptive tensions, however, are those which come because of changes in the individuals' careers and lifestyles, those dealing with the routines and pressures of continued living together (including discovering unanticipated things about one's spouse), and the many problems associated with growing older. As couples move through married life they are bound to experience repeated crises, among them the famous "seven-year itch" that comes at almost any time, when the curiosity of what it would be like living with someone else sets in.

UNDERGOING CHANGE

One of the best ways of looking at the evolution of a marriage is to set it in the context of the developmental stages in the lives of the people involved. In a fascinating work entitled *Passages*, Gail Sheehy shows how adults seem to move through stages of development similar, in many ways, to the developmental stages of childhood. Her framework can also be used to show how the stages of development in individuals' lives are bound to affect their marriages—shaping them, changing them, sometimes destroying them.

Of course, a marital relationship goes through stages of development itself. The formal decision to marry can come during any one of them, sometimes prematurely, as I have already said. There is courtship, romance, settling in. There is the getting-acquainted stage, the entrance-of-children stage, and adjustments required when they leave home or when one's work life outside the home changes. There are problems around the development of habits and routines. There are dead points, when the excitement and movement of the relationship seems to have gone. Beyond (or above) all these there may come a time of "reromancing" and a positive new experiencing of each other in the relationship. For a couple who makes it, there is a richness to the later years which makes the term "Golden Anniversary" have real meaning.

In a *New York* magazine article published before her book, called "Catch-30 and Other Predictable Crises of Growing Up Adult," Sheehy describes an interview she had with a television newscaster. The man was well-known, highly salaried, handsome, and, at 46, at the peak of his professional life. But he was not happy. Since teenage, he had been driven by a desire to be successful. He had achieved his desire, professionally, but his personal life was a mess. He had not been able to successfully integrate the two.

The newscaster's dilemma is a common one. Many people, after having reached their middle years—the years when they were supposed to have "made it," the years when their lives were supposed to have ripened into balance—find that being "grown up" does not bring with it the happiness and security they had been taught to expect. The problem is that the realities of most people's lives don't square with the myth of maturity. One does not become an adult, finally "grow up," and that's it. The years of adult life are no more static and unchanging than the years of youth.

It would be to our advantage to drop the myth of maturity, as suggested by the O'Neills and others, and begin to look at the adult years in the same kind of developmental ways we've learned to look at the years of childhood. It doesn't work well for people to cover up the changes going on inside themselves with masks of "grown-upness" or façades of success if they have not come to grips with the meaning of these changes. Adults are not the same from year to year, nor are their relationships. Much of the discomfort felt by adults in mid-marriage or mid-career is not the fault of defects in character, as marital moralists often put it. It is linked to normal changes in the attitude and feelings of people as they move along through life and as the situations in which they find themselves, such as their work, affect them in new ways.

STAGES OF DEVELOPMENT

Erik Erikson was the first person to discuss adult life in terms of stages of development. He saw the 20s as the stage of *Intimacy*. The problem of people in their 20s was to somehow get through the "shoulds" of spousehood and parenthood and to achieve a genuine and self-preserving intimacy. Many, he observed, never made the breakthrough. For those who did, and were able to be generally successful in the rest of their lives, their 40s and 50s were the stage of *Generativity*. It was at this point, with their children grown, that people were freed to be able to develop concern for the new generation. Finally, in the stage of *Ego Integration*, people could come to grips with their finitude, give up whatever wishes they might have had that things had been different, and finish what work they could in moving toward the personal goals remaining in their lives.

Erikson's analysis is a good beginning, but it does not go far enough. The stages through which adults pass are far more complex then he suggested. Every decade of life brings with it new problems and confusions. Gail Sheehy remembers her former husband coming home on the night of his thirtieth birthday. He sat at the kitchen table with a raincoat over his T-shirt. When she asked him what was going on, he said that he was waiting to become a "dirty old man." It's from the situation in which he found himself, and the one in which she found herself in response, that the title for her article came. Because of the things happening in their individual lives their marriage was put in a double bind from which it never recovered.

In reading Sheehy's article I found myself reliving my own life. All of the stages she described were ones I had either experienced or watched others move through.

The first stage of adulthood, according to Sheehy, comes approximately between the ages of sixteen and twenty-two. (In all of the stages she describes she found a leeway of plus or minus a couple of years.) This first stage is the one of *Pulling Up Roots*—when people say they want to get away from their parents but resist doing it because they still feel safely a part of the family in which they grew up. About midway through the stage, a person begins teetering on the fence and seeks out peers for help in escaping from family ties. The chief fear of this stage is that the person is still a child who cannot take care of himself or herself. Because of this, there is a lot of acting-out as a cover-up for the fear. More important, there is often the seeking out of a partner to perform the soothing functions formerly provided by the family. One of the major problems of this stage is not being able to cut the ties to one's parents. Some are never able to do this, and at forty or fifty they are still worried about how their parents will feel about their behavior.

Following this stage, for those who get through it, is the one that comes between the ages of approximately twenty-two and twenty-nine, the stage of *Provisional Adulthood*. According to Sheehy it's during this stage that people first seriously experiment with getting into the adult world, trying to build their own lifesystems. The strong commitments and bravado typical of people in this stage of development often cover an unsureness about whether or not they can truly be adults. There is a lot of parent-weaning going on during this stage and a lot of attaching to mentors. It's a time of life in which people feel many new "shoulds." At the same time they are struggling to discover the authentic intimacy of which Erikson writes. All of which means that this stage is a scary one. It is a time when conflict grows between wanting to hold onto commitment and at the same time feeling frustrated because it is impossible to experiment and explore.

It's out of such feelings of frustration that the next stage develops. Between the ages of twenty-nine and thirty-two comes the *Age Thirty Transition*. All of a sudden the "big" question becomes: "What is life all about, anyhow?" Many people, during this stage, go through what Gail Sheehy and her husband did, a complete tearing up of the lifestyles and goals they had created for themselves. It is a time of exciting new visions or shattered expectations. It is a time of marital conflict and divorce, or a time of breaking through into tremendous new possibilities. No matter what else, it is a time of deep concern about where one is going in life. This represents a challenge to marriage as strong as any the relationship ever will have to endure, since it is a time when one and/or the other of the partners may feel it necessary to completely redirect his or her life without consideration of the effect of this on the other. It is because of this that there arises the double-bind, the "Catch-30," in which Gail Sheehy found herself.

According to Sheehy, a typical Catch-30 situation would go something like this: The husband has finally gained enough experience to have some idea of what his professional future is going to be. He has a growing sense of competency at what he is doing but apprehension about the meaning of it all. He gets more and more wrapped up in thinking about what he *should* be doing. His wife, meanwhile, is feeling something similar. As her husband becomes more self-centered she begins to pay more attention to herself. She wants either to begin to develop a career of her own, free from dependency on him, or to have him shift more of his attention away from his job and back to her and their children. This creates a tension. He doesn't want to have to worry about her. He would like to see her go back to school, or move ahead in her profession, or get into volunteer work, or whatever. He cares about her, but wants to be free of her dependence. He is too involved with his own concerns to be able to think about her development. What she picks up from this, however, is a lack of caring.

What happens in situations like this is a shift in signals. The man stops wanting a substitute mother to take care of him. What he wants instead is a companion who understands him. But what he thinks of as encouragement for his wife's own development, she may perceive of as a threat—a wish to be free of her. Meanwhile, the wife, who has been the nurturer in the relationship, finds confusing feelings bubbling inside of her. This is especially true if she is a woman who thought of marriage, when she began it, as her "profession." Women who begin marriage with this kind of outlook don't expect to have to function outside the home in a full sense. They usually see themselves as being like their own mothers. As long as their husbands are satisfied with this, things are fine. But if their husbands change their expectations, the wives are likely to feel betrayed. It's the same as being shoved back to adolescence and having to go through adulthood all over again. If such a woman isn't able to summon up the courage to begin again, the double-bind tightens. If she retreats into her former role, he rebels. If she wants to begin again he's unconcerned. It's a Catch-30.

Fortunately, most couples have the patience and the trust in each other to see this stage as only temporary. According to Sheehy, the next stage, the stage of *Rooting*, comes between the ages of thirty-two and thirty-nine, although there is a bit of leeway on either side. Life, by this time, seems more stable. By their late 30s, people are the same older parents they remember their parents as being. They've got the energy that goes with recognition and reasonable success. It now seems possible to shape their visions into concrete goals. Family life is settling down and they can be more relaxed. At least this is so for some. For others, there is an inner shrug of quiet desperation. At thirty a person is not yet able to predict where he or she will end up. By forty there is more certainty. If the person has made it, the problem is taking the steps necessary to move ahead. If the person has fallen short, vision must be reduced downward or other directions found to keep one from sinking into boredom or depression.

The late 30s lead to another time of change, the *Mid-Life Transition*. This is often a time of acute discomfort as people wait for their hopes and fears to come true. But it can be a rich time, too. I've celebrated more than one bang-up fortieth birthday party. I remember getting a letter from a good friend who had been afraid turning forty would somehow mean the end of her youth. But when the day actually came, a remarkable thing happened. She wrote:

And this morning I am 40!

I find . . . that it feels good!

I feel like I have arrived somewhere—come out onto a high open space (that's a bit overdrawn, but it *is* an expansive feeling) and it's not an empty plateau at all—lots of other people around who got here sooner, and now I'm here too—what do you know! Forty, and it looks like there are lots of years ahead, with lots that can be done in them . . .

Wow.

I'll tell you one thing—it's a heck of a lot better than 39, which was no-wheresville.

Silly, all this. If we didn't keep track, today wouldn't feel any different from any other day. But that would be too bad. I'd be sorry to miss the good feeling of today.

You know, I almost feel like a kid does on his birthday—bigger.

Surviving this transition, feeling "bigger" as my friend did, sends one into what Sheehy calls the stage of *Restabilization and Flowering*. For the people able to weather the Mid-Life Transition, this is perhaps the best time of all. It is often the best time in a marriage. Those who have made it to this stage feel autonomous, competent, unafraid, ready to be the generative, ego-integrated people of whom Erikson wrote.

Of course not all marriages and not all people "flower," as

Sheehy puts it, in their forties and fifties. But later years are not as fearsome as our youth-oriented culture might lead us to believe. There was a documentary on television called "Male Menopause—The Pause That Perplexes." It talked about the effects of the Mid-Life Transition on men. One of the men in the film was in his mid-fifties. After listening to the complaints of other men in a discussion group his turn finally came. He said: "I'm fifty-five and feel great. I know now I've got fewer years to go than the ones behind. That's O.K. I feel good about me and I'm going to take advantage of all the time I've got left. There's nothing I have to be anymore except me. I intend to live every day fully, until the day I die."

To reach this point in life the man had to pass through many stages. During some of them he felt good about himself and where he was going. During others he felt pain. He got where he was by accepting the realities of his life and dealing with them and his feelings about them one-by-one. If there is something like a male menopause, he certainly demonstrated that there is nothing more to fear in it than there is in the menopause experienced by women. Both are things that happen as stages through which one can pass to greater freedom.

I have been careful to avoid the use of the word "maturity" in what I have been saying. I believe that many people do things prematurely. They move before it is appropriate to do so. This includes moving into marriage, and moving out of it. But I also believe that it is a mistake to believe that something is wrong in our lives if we move through periods of pain, turmoil, and confusion. There is no way to avoid this. Adults are bound to pass through predictable stages of life. Each of the stages has within it its own tasks. The crises encountered in them, though they are often confusing and painful, are good and necessary. It is in dealing with them that we learn and grow. Our goal should not be to avoid crises, but to en-counter them creatively, knowing that they have a role to play in our development. Knowing that the problems of one stage of development are often unique to it can certainly help a couple who find their marriage strained by the forces of their personal developmental lives.

Looking at life in a developmental way has helped me. While it did not save a marriage, it let me put my first marriage into the kind of perspective that allowed me to understand its problems and to feel able to recommit myself to another marriage when the appropriate time came. I pulled up roots, struggled free of my ties to home, tried out several models of adulthood in my 20s, went through the stage of being the bastard in a Catch-30 trap, then came out of it into a period of rootedness, feeling good about myself both personally and professionally. I am now looking forward to moving through whatever transitions lie ahead to the years of stability and flowering yet to come. I have no intention of being the dirty old man Gail Sheehy's former husband fantasized himself becoming as he faced the first major transition period of his life.

It's silly to kick and scream and to try to be what we are not as we pass through the various stages of our lives. To do so is to seriously risk damaging the relationships about which we care most, such as our marriages. It doesn't matter if we are thirty or ninety: we are never going to be fully "mature." What we have to do is live as open selves, as the O'Neills suggest in their second book, *Shifting Gears*. We have to be open in the full sense of what they have always meant by this term: open to ourselves, open to our spouses, open to others, and open to new experiences. We need to adopt a stance, such as that of Carl and Helen Rogers, in which we see our relationships as opportunities for growth, as aids to dealing with the problems of our developing selves. If we can understand that the stages we are to go through are natural and not pathological, we will see that each means there is something else to follow—and that it's worthwhile to hang in and see what happens.

The pledge that a couple ought to be making, when they decide to enter into marriage, is not that they will have no problems to overcome, or that they will always be in tune with each other, or that they will have no Catch-30 experiences. Instead, they should bet that they can stick by each other, understanding what's going on in the other even when it's neither something they like nor something they can change.

10

Breaking Points and Beyond

In spite of all the alternatives being lived out by people today, there is no question that ours is still a marriage-oriented society. The majority of adults will marry at some time or another, and the majority of them will remain married. Counseling agencies and individuals such as I, who do marital counseling, will always try to provide what help we can to those who want to be able to work out problems in their marriages. But this doesn't mean that all people should stay married.

In describing how people enter into a marriage relationship, I have used the image of jumping off a cliff. I have suggested that a couple can fly beautifully together if they will work at it. But I've also suggested that it's wise to carry along a parachute, just in case things don't work so well. The parachute represents that bundle of skills, strengths, and supportive structures that a person can use to cushion the fall that comes after a couple reaches a breaking point that can't be healed. Because it can be difficult to develop these skills, strengths, and structures at the last minute, it seems important to discuss them in a serious exploration of the marriage option.

DECIDING TO END IT

Sometimes, as hard as it may be for a couple to admit it, the best solution to an inability to work out problems is to end the relationship. While the intention of a couple entering marriage ought to be to build a continuing and growing relationship, they ought not to think of marriage as an institution to which they should be bound *no matter what*. It is wrong to assume that a couple can solve *any* problem. Unfortunately, neither the "sacredness" of marriage nor the insights of marriage counseling have magic to them. Nor is maintaining the façade of marriage in the face of hostility or psychological separation a caring or intelligent thing to do. The question that must always be answered in a troubled marriage is not "why get divorced?"—a couple can always come up with answers to that. The question instead is "why stay married?" If there is not a good answer to *this* question—if the partners have lost respect for one another, have become intolerant of each other's lifestyles, have come to feel that the weight of the defects of their relationship overpowers its assets, have lost the willingness to continue working on their problems, or simply have no spark left in their relationship and no love— then it may be time for them to reconsider the value of staying together.

It is not easy for a couple to do this. It is bound to involve them in a painful process accompanied by a good deal of loneliness and self-doubt. If there are children, not only are there concerns about them, but there are fears of what it would be like to be a single parent, or to have to live apart from them. For a woman contemplating divorce, if she hasn't established a career outside the home, there are fears of financial insecurity compounded by apprehensions about her ability to take over the roles her husband had performed in the family. For a man contemplating divorce there is the need to replace his wife's skills and companionship. For both, there is the need to overcome the anger they feel toward their ex-spouse or the damage to their pride that comes from being rejected or from being unable to continue a relationship with someone they have valued. No one wants to think of himself as a failure, especially a failure at human relationships; most people mean it when they pledge themselves to each other at the beginning of a marriage. All of these factors make it difficult to avoid feelings of self-pity, guilt, resentment, and a lingering hope that things will get better if only the person and his or her spouse will try harder. Such feelings keep many couples together long after whatever was good in their relationship has died. They are unable to translate the traditional wedding vow of "as long as we both shall live" into something more constructive, like "as long as we both shall love."

BEING CARE-FULL OF DIVORCE

If a couple cannot live well together, divorce may be the most caring thing for them to do. But they should be as care-full in thinking about divorce as they should have been in thinking about marriage in the first place. They should examine their motives and needs as deeply as they can to be sure of their meaning.

Any time people find themselves involved in a hurtful relationship something is the matter with one, the other, or both of them. No matter what the "matter" is, it had better be examined if the troubled spouse expects to carry on with life in a fruitful way. Ending a relationship may take pressure off a troubled spouse, but it is unlikely to be a solution to his or her own problems. A poor marriage may be the result of a bad choice of partners or of unmatched shifts in the lifestyles of the people involved, but if marital problems are a reflection of deeper problems within one or both of the partners, then they had better seek outside help. Their marriage may not be saved, but without such help it is unlikely that those troubled are going to be any better off in the future.

All right. Let's assume that the couple has sought whatever advice and therapy they can. They have tried to work out their problems, but things seem no better. They have tried to find alternative behaviors within their marriage, but it has not seemed to make any difference in the way they feel. If all this has been done, the best thing they can do is to trust what is inside of themselves. If they are honest and sensitive, they usually both *know* and *feel* when the time for a separation has come. The centered relationship essential to marriage no longer exists. It may even be recognized that it never really did.

The question then—the question that follows an absence of a good answer to "why stay married?"—is "what is the most caring thing to do?" The couple may decide to make some sort of accommodation within their marriage, even though they would be happier apart. A lot of people do this. The couple may decide to remain legally married but undertake a *de-facto* separation because of what others will think about them, because of their insecurity or pride, or because they think it will be the best thing for their children—much is done, wrongly, in the name of all of these things. The couple may decide that the wisest and most caring thing they can do is to divorce.

A divorced or divorcing person's life should be seen in the same light as anyone else's. No matter what our marital status, we are all due respect, acceptance, and privacy. Neither as individuals looking at others in the situation, nor as individuals in the situation ourselves, should we want there to be a choosing of sides—though this is almost impossible to prevent. Marriage is a relationship and what happens in the relationship is seldom the "fault" of just one partner. Everyone involved in a divorce needs support, understanding, and acceptance. People within the situation can help those who are outside by being both honest with them and undemanding. It is especially important not to demand they cast blame or share negative feelings about the other person in the divorce or that they join in scapegoating someone else, like "the lover." For those outside the situation it is important to hang in with the divorcing ones in spite of their anger and pain. In our case, without the caring of the many people around us with whom we felt in community, my former wife and I could never have moved through divorce in the almost friendly way we did.

PATTERNS OF DIVORCE

There are as many patterns for divorce as there are for marriage, but they tend to fall into three categories. The most common, unfortunately, is the *nasty divorce*, in which there is an accusation of fault. Blaming fans hostility in the spouse blamed and breeds counterhostitily. Societal attitudes encourage such an approach. Most divorce laws, although this is beginning to change, have been written as though divorce would never be necessary unless one of the spouses had done something wrong, like committing adultery. Only in a few states has it been recognized that divorce may not be a "fault" situation at all. There is no "wrongdoing" in a couple's recognizing that it is more caring for them to end a bad relationship than to continue it.

The sort of divorce recommended by those of us who are idealists is a *friendly divorce*. In such a separation the individuals involved let bygones be bygones and turn from feeling resentful and hostile to attending to the needs of their children, if they have any and their about-to-be-former spouses. A friendly divorce is one that is seen by a couple as a positive step toward a future that will be better for all involved.

It may be too much to expect a couple to remain friendly while moving through the pain of a divorce, however. If the people involved try to maintain a pretense of friendliness when they don't feel it, it may be worse than being openly hostile, since the repressed anger is bound to erupt in other ways. Bernard Steinzor, who writes out of his personal experience as a marriage counselor, suggests that a *reasonable divorce* may be the best we can expect from people. In such a separation the divorcing couple forgets about trying to be friendly, but avoids being nasty by granting each other freedom in divorce, agreeing to act in a reasonable and civil manner.

THOUGHTS ABOUT THE CHILDREN

Most people who are unhappily married try to hide their unhappiness from others. Such attempts to cover up feelings are, more often than not, harmful to the people involved. It is better to let the underlying bitterness and hostility of a bad relationship come out into the open where it can at least be recognized for what it is and dealt with. Children are often used as an excuse for not doing this. But people do not really protect children by trying to deceive them. Children are quick to pick up on the feelings underlying their parents' behavior.

To attempt to deceive children is to use them for one's own reasons—such as wanting to be loved or respected in a way no longer possible with a spouse. Even worse is showering too much love on a child because the spouse rejects it. This may turn the child into a person who expects such unilateral love from others in the future. The fact is that no child can avoid being caught up in his or her parents' problems when they reach the point of considering divorce. But, then, there is little way for children to avoid being affected by *any* of their parents' major problems. At the time of divorce it is important to be honest with children at their own level of understanding; that is, answering their questions at the time they are asked. It is also important to assure children that, divorce or not, they will not be deserted and that the problems necessitating the separation were created by the parents, not the children. Since children come into the lives of their parents without ever choosing to do so, the parents who choose to have children have a permanent responsibility to them—a responsibility not dissolvable through divorce.

If children can be shown that they will not be deserted and that they are not the cause of the problem—and if a divorce can be moved through in freedom, without recrimination or nastiness—then there is no reason to believe that the children involved won't be better off than if their parents tried to stay together "for the children's sake." Divorce is a way of clearing away the "emotional smog" which is usually smothering the family of a disturbed marriage. My experience in counseling suggests that although the breakup of a marriage requires major readjustments, including significant economic hardships, especially for women, few of the people who take initiative in divorce regret their decisions. I find their children, on the whole, to be less disturbed living with the single parent than they had been living in the troubled marriage. Children whose parents live together in a satisfying relationship are less likely to be disturbed than those whose parents divorce, but living with a divorced parent is not necessarily the breeder of neurosis and delinquency some have suggested.

One advantage of divorce for the children of troubled marriages is that it lets them form their own opinions of their parents, unobstructed by the veils a parent is bound to throw up in front of himself or herself in times of strife. Such children will have to endure conflicts of loyalty and love, but in coming to understand why their parents had to choose as they did, children learn to appreciate and value their parents' different personalities and needs. It gives them an opportunity to experience their parents in ways impossible for those children whose parents pretend to be what they are not. All of this assumes, of course, that the divorced spouses don't try to infect the children with all of their own negative feelings about one another. It also assumes that the spouses don't try to pass off a false positive image of each other. Children are bound to see through this; it is worse than being honestly negative—something from which at least the children can learn.

Thus the end of a marriage, if it is moved through in a respectful way, is a better example for children than the faking of love tried by parents afraid of what effects a divorce might have. It is only in seeing adults who are honest with their feelings that children can learn how to be honest with their own feelings and to respond to the feelings of others. The worst example of all is failing to admit mistakes. Attempts at deception are bound to leave children confused and unsure about how to deal with their own feelings and mistakes. Most of the disturbance in the children of divorce comes not from the fact of their parents' separation, but from their parents' difficulty in honestly and openly dealing with problems.

A lot more could and should be said about the effects of divorce on children and about the problems of continued parenting after a separation has come. Earl Grollman's two books, *Explaining Divorce to Children* and *Talking About Divorce*, are perhaps the best books yet written on the subject. In addition, having spent many years as an advisor to the Parents Without Partners organization, I would recommend it as a helpful support group for divorced or divorcing parents. PWP offers single parents the chance to share with each other insights about raising children without the help of a spouse. Through both local meetings and its national magazine, *The Single Parent*, PWP offers the best professional advice available to the support of its members. I would even urge parents considering divorce to contact their local PWP chapter. It will provide good reality testing of the implications of the choice they are contemplating.

THE CELEBRATION OF DIVORCE

A lot of my time as a minister is taken up with the problem of marriage, especially the problems of getting into and out of it. Of course, getting into it is a lot easier and a lot happier than getting out. Not only is the choice to end a marital relationship filled with the sorts of problems already discussed, but the mechanics themselves are difficult, and very different from those of marriage. One's consultant is an attorney, rather than a minister. Arrangements to divide property, family, and income have to be argued out and be acceptable to both the couple and a third party, a judge. It is a painful, sorrowful, and often hateful experience, with little friendliness or even respect.

One problem of divorce is that there is no rite of transition into the new ways of life chosen by the couple, no way for the two people to affirm themselves as they now wish to be—no equivalent to the wedding with which they began their marriage. As for ministers, though they often counsel people about the problems of marriage and divorce, there is no role for them to play, and no role for the community of their church to play, when a marriage ends. At least for members of its own religious family, a church could fulfill a needed healing ministry if it were to provide a rite of transition for the ending of marriage comparable to the one it provides for the beginning. Since this book is an attempt to address the option of marriage in its full cycle, beginning with its celebration, it seems appropriate to talk about the end, if an end must come, and to consider how *it* ought to be celebrated.

Both my wife and I have been divorced and remarried. In fact, ironically, she was one of my brides once, as I officiated at her first wedding. After our marriages had begun to fall apart we met again, this time person to person, rather than minister to bride. We had to move through a lot to come to our decision to wed, but we did so, and happily. We chose to share our vows privately, with only two close friends and the minister present. Then we announced what we had done to a gathering of friends we had invited to share in "A Rather Happy Occasion." The decision to formalize our relationship required a lot of thought and was based on a knowledge about ourselves and a sureness about our decision developed over a long period of time spent living together. The considerations talked about in this book were very much a part of our thinking.

My former wife and I were separated for an equally long period of time before our divorce became final. Our decision to separate and then to divorce was based on a similarly deep knowledge about ourselves and the reality of our relationship. It was a decision based on respect and entered into with good will, even if it was not an altogether happy decision for either of us.

We tried, as best we could without specifically thinking about it, to work out a rite of sorts when it came time for formal divorce proceedings. It took place with the sharing of a meal with our children and the two people who were eventually to become our new partners. Just as with the sharing of vows between Jan and me, this was a private time for the people involved—a special time, the specialness of which was marked by the meal. To an outsider what happened would probably not have seemed like a rite at all. But, simple as it was, it placed our decision in a larger context and allowed our children and those closest to us to recognize us in our new ways of life. The minutes in court the next day were not made any easier by what we did—the judge's words granting a petition of divorce were as traumatically final as a minister's "You are wed"—but we did provide ourselves with a way of moving from an unhappy moment to a new pair of lives in which happiness was possible.

Others have moved through their divorce in ways similar to ours, but many are forced to move through it alone, without support, without rituals to help. This is a shame, because what we did has helped us in living our separate, yet still often related, lives. There are other people, however, who have taken what we did a step further and have gone through a formal marriage-ending ritual in a church, with invited guests, just like a wedding. This may sound bizarre, at first, but it doesn't have to be. Divorce needn't be filled with sadness. As I've suggested, it can be entered into caringly, as a positive act. My former wife and I chose to end our marriage of fourteen years and to establish new relationships. But we didn't do this in rejection of each other. We did it because it was no longer appropriate to continue relating to one another within a marriage.

Many wedding ceremonies carry the passage from the Old Testament that begins with the words: "To everything there is a season." It is a passage which would be even more appropriate to a rite of divorce. It takes a while to get used to the idea of being in the same place with a former spouse who is no longer "yours"—of being autonomous people in spite of your histories—but it can be done. Not only that, it feels good to be able to be in the company of someone with whom you have shared a difficult process like divorce and to be free of the bad feelings of the experience. So why not a ceremony recognizing, even celebrating, such a choice?

One reason why not is that our perception of the end of marriage has been so long conditioned by fault. Feelings about this will continue long after no-fault divorce laws have done away, legally, with the need for accusation. This makes it difficult to conceive of divorce as something other than the recognition of failure or, at best, the death of a relationship. The normal view of marriage, supported by all the surroundings of the picture-book ideal as it's been discussed, is of a decision made for a lifetime. The fact is, though, that marriages don't die; their reasons for being cease to be. Failure and fault are poor ways of thinking about how this happens—and lifetimes are for living out well, not unhappily.

THE ROLE OF THE CHURCH

Organized religion has to bear a good deal of the responsibility for the unhappiness experienced by people with troubled marriages. Orthodox religious groups claim that marriage is "an institution ordained by God in the very nature of our beings," and intended to last until death. Some faiths, such as the Roman Catholic, while recognizing divorce, are unwilling to recognize remarriage, since in God's eyes marriage should be once and for all. Not only do I disagree with this, I would go beyond it to say that religious groups ought to be anxious to join in the affirmation of a positive choice of divorce if a couple is able to accept their choice as that. To do so would be to value caring and to symbolize the couple's commitment to something greater than just the concern for one another with which their marriage began—their commitment to life itself and to living their lives in the richest and happiest ways possible.

For a religious group to sanction rites of divorce would be to say to divorcing people that there are positive and affirming ways to approach the end of a marriage and to move into new lives. It would give divorcing people, as well as their families and friends, support in seeing what they are doing as something best for all of them—something about which they can feel good. Anyone who has been through a divorce without such support knows how helpful it would be. It would not only require of the divorcing people the same sort of seriousness of intention required of people choosing to celebrate marriage in a wedding, it would also ask of the surrounding community of family and friends the same pledge of friend-ship and support the two people sought when originally being wed. It would provide an opportunity to forgive, the most difficult thing of all for divorcing people and those around them. Not only would the couple then have the chance to forgive each other, but they could forgive those around them for not providing the help and support they needed earlier, if such forgiveness were called for. The community, in turn, would be able to forgive the couple for their hurting and abuse of others when the pain and turmoil of their own lives was too great to contain. Finally, the rite of divorce would provide a way of sharing a blessing with the two people as they embark upon new lives apart. It would transform the moment of divorce from a burial service for something dead into a celebration of hope for what can be.

Taking part in such a ceremony, even informally in the privacy of one's home, wouldn't be easy. It would require the couple to honestly care about one another and the well-being of each in their new lives. But that ought to be the way the end of a relationship should come about. I have yet to see a hostile or uncaring divorce in which everyone involved wasn't hurt. If we could provide some sort of mechanism, whether a formal one, such as suggested above, or an informal one, such as used by my former wife and me, it would at least symbolize to others that there is a caring way to end a marriage, just as there is a caring way to begin one.

I wish no one ever had to divorce—that all marriages were "made in heaven" and would last beautifully for a lifetime. But they aren't and never will be. As many as one out of every three marriages begun today will end in divorce. I don't argue that we should feel good about this, but it may not be as negative a sign as most people assume. Maybe the increase in divorce does not mean that marriage is losing its value, but that people are becoming more care-full in their relationships—trying to be more full of care for themselves and the people with whom they relate. In many cases, divorce *is* the most caring thing that can be done. Though it may be difficult to approach the ending of a marriage with such a perspective, it is far better that divorce be undertaken as an act of caring than as an act of vengeance, an admission of failure, or a recognition of fault.

The choices people make about their lives are their own. No one can say that someone else should end a marriage. What we can say, however, is that two people ought never to cease to care for one another, even if they cease to love. This thought ought to be in all our parachutes when we take the leap into marriage.

Preventing Divorce

Even though divorce may be the best alternative for a marriage that has become destructive, the question remains whether it is the *only* one. The answer is no. But the individuals in a troubled marriage do owe it to themselves to consider divorce, if they are not able to come up with positive reasons for remaining married. In saying this I am not trying to devalue marriage. On the contrary, I am placing as much value on marriage as I can. But to be valued marriage must be seen as a positive option.

THREAT OF DIVORCE

My experience in counseling suggests that a radical shift has taken place in our society in the past decade or so. As Margaret Mead puts it, we are in the midst of an epidemic of divorce. Our society now accepts divorce as a solution to an unhappy marriage. People who a few years ago never would have dared to think of ending their marriages—politicians, religious leaders, educators, public figures of all sorts—are divorcing in droves. When the announcement is made, it's barely mentioned in the press. It is no longer news for a public personality to end a marriage. In some parts of the country there is one divorce, now, for every two marriages.

This book, itself, could be taken as a further addition to the forces working in our society to undermine the permanency of marriage. It, after all, speaks about divorce in a noncondemning way as part of an overview of the marriage option. But it would have been dishonest for me, either personally or professionally, to pass over divorce in a book about marriage. It would be equally wrong, however, to imply that it is the only option, or even the best option, for people facing marital conflict.

Divorce should be the last alternative for a couple, a final act of caring when all else has proven inadequate. I can personally testify to the fact that those who do it will never be totally free of negative feelings—feelings of guilt and regret. There has been no more painful time in my life than the evening when I sat down to dinner with my children and told them that it was the last night I would be spending with them in that house. If I had ever thought my marriage would result in such a decision, and that I would have to endure that agony, I never would have entered into the marriage in the first place. No matter how happy I am now, that pain remains. In a less permissive society, the recognition of what that pain would be like and the existence of social pressures on a person in a position such as mine probably would have been enough to dissuade me from leaving my first marriage. But it would also have kept me from discovering what a good marriage begun in a knowing maturity could be like.

PRESERVING

Of course, if one can sustain a marital relationship in a positive way, the pain of such a choice may never have to be endured. Giving consideration to the ways one might enhance the health of a relationship as it goes along is far better than trying to figure out what to do after a breaking point has been reached. If partners can enrich the positive aspects of their relationship they will be able to deal with tensions *before* the tensions become overly destructive. A couple open with each other and in touch with feelings will be able to deal with negative clues when they surface—while they can still be identified with their source. To let negative feelings go without doing anything about them is to give them a chance to fester and explode with a violence magnified in the process. I've tried to show how destructive and unpredictable outbreaks of anger and hostility can be when they are not a direct response to whatever stimulated them in the first place. So, to repeat, the best strategy for maintaining the health of a relationship is for those involved to be open, honest, and caring, combining a hard-headed thoughtfulness with a soft-hearted concern.

A second preventive measure important for preserving the health of a relationship is a combining of caring for oneself with caring for the other. "Love thy neighbor as thyself," says the Bible. The biblical editors were very selective about what they included in the canon and what they filtered out. For them this statement summed up what it meant to love God. The passage points to a reality often forgotten by non-carers. Not only is love of life made real only in love of others, but there can be no separation of love of self from love of others. We can throw up all sorts of protections in an attempt to deceive ourselves about our lovingness or the need to be loving, but there is no way to love ourselves if we cannot care about others.

Just as we can't be lovable without being loving, so we cannot be caring unless we are willing to care for ourselves. If we don't care for ourselves then we have nothing to give. What we have to give is what we are, not just something ephemeral, like loving feelings. Feelings are important, but the person with whom we share love is a whole person. It is from interacting in depth with the wholeness of his or her personhood that we are enabled to grow and to become more. In turn we have that moreness to share back. The joy of our continuing relationship is the *all* of what happens between two people, not just the feelings we have for each other.

Paying attention to oneself—to one's own growth and well-being—is, then, essential to a relationship. Not only do those who feel bad about themselves increase their own vulnerability, but they act as an emotional drain on others. Those who are dependent on others for their sense of worth are going to be threatened by all sorts of things that would be no threat to secure people. And those who are depended upon are liable to become deeply resentful of their dependent spouses and to yearn for freedom. If you have not experienced how it feels to be in a dependent relationship, try the Gestalt exercise of having someone lean on you while standing back to back, and then reverse positions. It's tiring either way you do it. Dependency is a major cause of marital unhappiness. It's far better for a couple to relate as free-standing, self-assured, self-secure individuals willing to be consciously and supportively *inter*dependent, rather than draining each other in an overly dependent way.

Dr. Theodore Rubin, in his excellent book *Compassion and Self-Hate*, says the key to self-care is to live compassionately with ourselves. This requires not only understanding and appreciating ourselves for what we are, but also valuing and wanting to take advantage of all of our unfulfilled potential. This is also the best way to enter into a relationship. I believe that what makes the relationship of my wife and me work so well is that we try to be ourselves. We carry into our relationship the following self-understanding, influenced by Rubin. It enhances what it is we have to share:

We are because we are. We exist and need no justification for our being. We are free and not just a function of the forces around us.

We are our real selves, not someone else's idea of what we ought to be, or our own fantasies. But we are also not yet fully what we can be. A lot of what we can be is yet to be discovered.

We need, we want, and we can choose. We are entitled to feelings and desires, though we need to remember that most of our wants are not needs. Much of what we want we don't need. There are things we would like we can do without.

We are where we are. We are at the center of our worlds and take ourselves wherever we go, even in our relationship—and that is the way it should be.

A third important thing to remember about preserving a relationship is that there is no relationship if partners are out of touch with each other. When two people disconnect, when they begin to move in their own directions without remaining in touch with each other, there is a serious risk that they will move too far apart to retouch. This does not mean that one has to give up autonomy and go along with, or give in to, the other. But unless one spouse can accept the other's moves *and* unless the acting spouse takes care not to move in ways harmful to the other, there will be problems. A marriage is a relationship shared in depth. What one partner does can never be thought of as only incidental to the relationship.

The clues that brought my second wife and me to the decision to formalize our marriage were a deep knowledge of each other and a deep feeling of commitment. This is something very different from trying to decide to be committed. We were sure. Neither of us had ever before been so sure about something that mattered so much. We were committed, but the commitment was not a decision we made. It was something we felt in the depth of our beings. War-weary veterans with no *need* to be married, no pressure to have to be so, we were able to make a *knowing* choice.

The continuation of that knowing is a key to the health of our relationship. It's what keeps us from trying to be deceptive with one another, although it is tempting to be so at times. There are things I cannot talk about with my wife, of course—such as confidences shared with me in counseling— and there are also some things in my personal life I'd rather keep private. But even if we do not share all the details of our lives, there are *no* significant feelings we keep hidden and no changes about which we are not open and clear. This is the most important protection against the disintegration of a relationship I know of.

Finally, there is a quality that must underlie all of what I have said—trust. Without partners trusting in each other's love, integrity, good will, and concern, a marriage will never be secure. Of course, trust depends on behavior. One must relate out of trust, then trust will grow as behavior affirms its value.

It is not easy to pay attention to all of these things at once, especially in a society in which it is now possible to join your minister, your senator, and your university president in walking away from a marriage. But paying attention and not walking away invests a marital relationship with a richness unmatched, I knowingly assert, by any of the many other lifestyles available.

Divorce is always possible. It may even become the most caring thing for a couple to do. But divorce never need have to be for those willing to resist marriage until they can maturely and knowingly enter into it—and who, then, respectfully and caringly nurture their relationship as a source of mutual enrichment and growth. Marriage as an option continues to stand the test in our permissive society not because it has to, but because of its continuing value and worth to those who knowingly and carefully choose it.

12

Older Yet Alive

During this past year my parents celebrated their Fiftieth Wedding Anniversary. It was a beautiful celebration put together by their children both as a note of thanks for all they have meant to us and as a mark of respect for the marriage they have held together through lots of ups and downs and some extremely difficult times. My parents are far from perfect, but the care and respect about which I have said so much has always been a part of their lives. It has let the later years of their marriage be as rich as the early years. Anyhow, that is the opinion of a grateful son. I appreciate my parents both for what they have been for me and what they have been for each other. It shows that the marriage option has value not just in its beginning, but also near its end.

THE YOUTH CONSPIRACY

The later years of a marriage and of life are not always so beautiful, though. At present there is a great gap between the generations—those in the middle try to be youthful and those who are young try to pretend they will never grow old. In her book *The Coming of Age*, Simone de Beauvoir speaks as a peer among the aging. She began to write when she realized how ashamed most people seem to feel about growing old. This attitude infects even those who have already grown to their later years; they join in a conspiracy of silence about what it means to be old, letting those younger get away with perpetuating stereotypes that tend to dehumanize the lives and marriages of older people.

114

To the degree that people are willing to join in such a conspiracy they are doomed to be affected by it as they grow older. This is particularly true for those who cannot afford the luxury of moving to the enclave of a retirement community where it is possible to create a separatist subculture. For most of the older folks left behind, at least those left behind in the kind of impersonal urban environments in which I have lived, there is isolation, loneliness, and depersonalization.

I'll have to admit that I am a product of such a culture. I once found it difficult to relate to people in their later years—I seldom had the chance to. The same has been true for many others. But such an analysis is not enough to account for the lack of involvement between the young and the old. Simone de Beauvoir says that just as there are destructive forces of racism and sexism in our society, so is there agism. Younger people come to dislike those older not only because they are more conservative and less open to change, but because the young fear growing older themselves. Modern young people, having lost their faith in traditional beliefs, such as life-after-death, are afraid of death and of losing their youth. At the same time they fear growing old, the young also aid in destroying the very qualities of life for older people they would wish to have present in their own later years: independence, vitality, and a worthwhile place in the general society. The conspiracy becomes a self-fulfilling prophecy, robbing the later years of the richness they deserve. The young tell the old that they cannot enjoy life and the old behave as though the young were right. That's why Golden Wedding Anniversaries can be so important. They speak not only to the people who've made it through all the years, but to those with all of them still to go. It's a small, symbolic way of breaking through the conspiracy.

THE MYTHS OF OLD AGE

To be old is not to be ugly or without feelings and desires. Some of the most beautiful love poetry, in fact, has been written by older people—such as Bertrand Russell, a lover in his 90s. Yet, one of the myths of old age is that to grow older is to lose one's sexual desire. An older person is even supposed to be "above" sex.

The fact is that older people are not without sexual desires, nor should they be. Dr. Elliott Feigenbaum, of the University of California Medical School at San Francisco, in a study of 600 people over 60, found that, while sexual drives and sexual facility decrease with aging, sexual feelings and wants are as much a part of the lives of older people as of those who are younger. He asked the people he interviewed how much sex they thought people of their age ought to have. The answers were mixed, as they would be for any age group, but they were summed up pretty well by one older man who said that when you are tired of looking at women, you are ready for the grave.

Feigenbaum argues in his study, which was published in the *New York Times*, that we must understand that older people have needs and feelings as deep and as strong as those of people who are younger. They are not sterile codgers beyond desire. Instead, Feigenbaum concluded, it is both normal and appropriate for older people to be interested in sex, and to desire a full intimacy of relationships. Lots of factors can inhibit either sexual drives or performance, but age, *per se*, is not one of them. I felt great after reading his article. I also felt good about the older people about whom I care, such as my parents. Age does not have to rob us of parts of ourselves important both to us and to our relationships.

Aging must cease to be seen by both the old and the not-yet-old as a time of disintegration. It would be a shame to consign older marrieds to a time of memory and inactivity—a shame both for those already older and those of us still on the way. Memories and the relaxation of old age can be pleasant, but memory decays and begins to unravel if there is no current aliveness to go with it. Indifference then follows, with a stifling effect on passions and activity.

We have all had the experience of being with delightful and vibrant older people. They are much more enlivening to me than many of my middle-aged peers. But we have also had the experience of being with older people who have given in to the myths of old age and have let stultifying habits become ingrained, taking the place of the curiosity and exploration necessary to keep life vibrant. Simone de Beauvoir calls this a parodying of one's former life. Writing as an older person herself, she says that the only way to avoid having one's later life be such a parody, or a time of decayed memories, is to go on pursuing the same interests and seeking to fulfill the same emotional needs as before. She says to her age peers that they ought to continue to be devoted to things that matter: people, causes, and creative effort. She asks them to break through the deadening conspiracy that encourages the elderly to serenely accept the pain and loneliness of old age, courageously enduring the years until the release of death. Such an agist attitude robs people of their humanity—of their wholeness as individuals. It asks those who are old to be spiritually, emotionally, and intellectually dead long before they die. That is not the way we should want to live our later years. Life in the later years should be no less rich than in the earlier ones. It should be a passionate time—a time to love and to care. Aging should not and need not quench emotions.

STAYING ALIVE

Preparing for one's later years, if one is to be emotionally as well as physically vital, has to include more than setting aside money, finding a retirement haven, and developing hobbies. It must also include the nurturing of involvements in life and a nurturing of relationships that will continue into later years. Most important, people must develop a sense of aliveness and celebration in which every moment is seen as an opportunity for experience.

As important as are the physical and economic problems of becoming old, it is one's ability or inability to be openly, curiously, and joyously alive that is the greatest problem of aging. This problem becomes acutely painful when one of the spouses in a marriage becomes dependently ill or dies. If the other spouse does not feel self-sufficient or has let go of his or her zest for life then the future does not hold out much hope.

As a minister I call on countless older people. The experiences of three of these people give a good example of how marriages are structured and what can happen when a spouse dies.

One of the people I used to visit was a woman in her late 80s. By the time I came to know her, her husband had been dead for six years. George and Mary had married in their teens. Both were the children of small merchants with little money to spare. Mary had delightful stories to tell about how the two of them rode street cars on dates and helped each other sneak away from their parents' stores so they could be together. They had beautiful dreams as young people. Mary's dreams included going to college, something few women did in her day. But she never fulfilled that dream. George found a job in an office and began his rise in the corporate world. It was almost a Horatio Alger story. He ended up as the president of one of the larger manufacturing companies in the community. While they had no children, Mary and George had many friends through his work and often visited with their families, though all their brothers and sisters eventually moved away to other cities. Mary remembers the retirement party for George, attended by the leading businessmen of the community, as a high point of their lives. She is proud of the fact that they still remember to send her cards at Christmas. Her biggest joy in life, now, is in telling her stories and poring over the scrapbooks she started when she first met George and began to dream of their marriage. There are a few pictures of nieces and nephews in the latest book, but the past six years fill only a couple of pages. As her few acquaintances from the old days drift away or die, her life becomes lonelier and lonelier. There wasn't much I could do by the time I came to know Mary except try to be with her in her memories and to help draw her into the present. Unfortunately, her life was too wrapped up in George's. When he died, so did she, though her body didn't recognize it until years later.

My second story is that of Ernest. Ernest had been the director of research for a corporation. He was highly respected, having made some of the major breakthroughs accomplished in his field. He was a friendly, self-assured, and generous man. His wife, who had died a couple of years before I met him, was remembered with affection by many people. Like George and Mary, they had traveled often, having no immediate family in the community. Ernest's retirement had been the occasion for a ceremony of recognition at least as auspicious as George's. The loss of his wife was a terrible blow to Ernest, coming soon after that fete. They had been a deeply devoted and loving couple, their marriage having survived a decade beyond their Golden Anniversary. The loss of his wife was not the end of life for Ernest, however. While devoted to her, he had dozens of interests to keep him occupied. He liked people, was easy to talk with, and was always a delight to be around. I remember his decision to take a cruise to the Mediterranean the year before he died. When I asked him what it was he wanted to see, he replied: "All the beauty of antiquity, and a few pretty women, too." Like Zorba the Greek, all of life was a green stone to this man.

Ernest's situation may seem an unfair one to compare to Mary's. He had advantages she did not have. He was skilled at being his own person, while she was not. Mary and George had structured their marital relationship in such a manner that she could not survive his death in a really fulfilling way. Ironically, without his helpmate, George might not have been able to manage either. I have seen many cases like this. The woman's movement has made a major point in showing how dehumanizing dependent relationships are to everyone involved, no matter how comforting they might seem; they result in people, like Mary, becoming dead long before their time.

Lest any of you who are Marys despair, however, let me describe the widowhood of another Mary—my own grandmother, Mary Leonard. The story of her youth and marriage is much like that of the other Mary. Her husband was one of those gallants who ran off to serve in the Spanish-American War. He sailed on a ship to Havana, where it fired off a round and turned for home, only to sink on the way, ending its career and leaving my grandfather with a lifetime of stories to tell and a love of the sea which he shared with us all. He was a proud man, and a strong man, although the Depression came close to breaking him, as it did so many others. His wife was proud, too—a lady, in the finest sense of the term. She was a beautiful woman at each stage of her life. But she was also a dependent women. Her husband wanted to provide, to take care of her, including doing most of the tasks of their household, after he retired.

I remember when I was told that my grandfather had cancer of the prostate. My family has always been good about being up front about things that matter, even such a painful thing as this. I watched, along with the others, as life seeped out of him. My grandmother tended him with love and care—and, more importantly, with dignity. She respected both him and herself too much to give in to behaving in any other way. After he died my grandmother didn't turn to her scrapbook, however. I can't even remember her having one, though she had good and loving memories of her husband. Mary Leonard blossomed out in the years after John died. She discovered things about herself that none of us had ever imagined. She made new friends, found new interests, and was a delight to be with. Somehow, even though there had been all the forms of dependency in their marriage, Mary Leonard managed to keep hold of her self-respect and her own personhood. On his part, in spite of all his needs, John had taken care not to crush her, either. She remained just as beautiful to him in their seventies as she had been when she was his young bride.

HUMANIZING LATER LIFE

Luckily for those of us who are younger there are more and more older people now living like Mary Leonard and like

Ernest. The Gray Panthers are coming to be an important force in some cities. In a less radical way the growing Senior Citizens Council Movement—better called "Gray Lib"—is giving older people an organized vehicle for demanding services and recognition. No longer do the elderly have to submit to a stereotype of powerlessness or accept the pittance of charity an otherwise uncaring society of younger people might provide to relieve itself of guilt. An interesting thing happens when people stop asking for things to be given to them out of the goodwill of their oppressors' hearts and start seizing their own freedom and organizing their own power. We are becoming an increasingly older society, and our older citizens are becoming less and less willing to accept being less than fully alive.

We who are younger must aid in this breakthrough to humanity for those who are older. But we must not do it in a pitying or conscience-ridden way. To care about the lives of people older, is, as well, to care about ourselves in our aging.

LATE MARRIAGE

A second aspect of the humanizing that has come with the rise of the Seniors' Movement has been the sanctioning of love and romance among those without partners in their later years. It was quite a shock to my family when my favorite aunt, an independent and strong person, announced that she had been proposed to in her sixty-someth year. There were a lot of family powwows over it, but Beulah went ahead. While it was not easy for her to readjust after her husband died, she had five good years with him. He was a fine man, a widower with a large family. Beulah found herself an instant grandmother with family to visit all over the country, which she did. I think she felt like a pioneer.

That was years ago. Today the situation is different. Older people are not only carrying on rich marriages, but they are initiating relationships capable of growing into the kind appropriate to celebrate with a wedding. In fact, more and more older couples are choosing the possibilities of marriage, rather than accepting the stereotype that this is somehow improper for older people who are, after all, "beyond" things like sexual feelings or a desire for intimacy.

As we have seen, the needs and desires of older people are as strong and as positive as those of the young. Because this is so, the elderly should feel free to marry, live together, or exercise any of the other options younger people might choose. Now that a movie has finally been made about Robin Hood and Maid Marion in their late 40s, it's time for a sequel to *Romeo and Juliet* for people in their 80s—and I don't mean to be funny.

Actually, I am acquainted with an older Romeo and Juliet of sorts—Jenny and Bill, who came to see me a few summers ago about the possibilities of a wedding. Theirs was a complicated situation. Not only were they both past fifty (and Bill twenty-six years older than Jenny—a gap difficult at any stage of life) but they had an unusual family tie. Bill was an uncle by marriage to Jenny. They had known each other for all of her conscious life. It was not until his wife died, however, that they had come to know each other fully enough for a friendship to develop. The friendship deepened to the point where they decided it would be appropriate to formalize it into a marriage. After talking with them it seemed to me that, in spite of all these complications, marriage was an appropriate expression of their relationship and ought to be celebrated with a wedding. Like the other couples in whose weddings I have shared, they wrote their own ceremony and celebrated it in the way most meaningful to them.

Recently I asked Jenny if she would be willing to reflect back on the decision she and Bill had made and to tell me what marriage has been like for them. In a somewhat edited version, here's what she had to say:

Sure, Bill and I were over fifty when we were married. I was just fifty and he was seventy-six. Just off the cuff I would say that when two people marry in their later years, especially if they have been married before as we had, they tend to accept their shortcomings better than younger folks. They remove rose-colored glasses that they wore for their earlier marriages. With age comes more patience and a desire to understand and tolerate. With children grown, they can concentrate more on their own interests and on each other than they could when the children were still at home.

I had always believed that a man past fifty would want a woman to lean on *his* strengths and to make no mention of his weaknesses. He would want her to show him and the world that she thought he was close to perfect and was worthy of being adored. He would need his ego bolstered more than a younger man. He would want her to make him feel young and handsome.

A women past fifty would, I thought, be looking for material support. She would want to be able to do her housework at leisure and not have to seek other employment to make ends meet.

Together, they would have saved enough money so that they could travel, buy the things they wanted, entertain and go out, and have no sweat over doctor bills and such. I thought most people over fifty would think of their husband-wife relationship as similar to that of a parent to a child: the man dominant and aggressive and the wife grateful to him for providing for her.

I sometimes feel that Bill would have been more at ease had he married someone who fit that picture better than I. But I don't fit it. I feel more like two generations removed from Bill's peers than being just twenty-six years younger than he is. This is because during the five years between my former marriage and the one to Bill I was in perfect tune with my children and their friends, a most unusual situation. I outgrew my need to be a mother and became friends with them. I was accepted 100 percent as I was. We were all "traitors," in a sense, to our own generations, but I loved living in "their world."

This remained rewarding to me until I saw, within the structure of our marriage, that my attitudes were a real threat to Bill's way of living. To make matters even more complicated, I am a Unitarian and a very liberal thinker. There was no way for me to pretend to be desperately dependent on my husband, as were women of earlier generations.

If you were including a chapter in this book of yours on great differences of age in marriage, I think that what I would have to contribute would be more appropriate than whatever I can say about marriage, itself, late in life. I don't find that being older has given us that much of a problem. But we have different values and different interests which are conditioned by the generations with which we identify. This *does* give us problems.

We have had long discussions about our differences. I think Bill would find it much more comfortable if I would just give up my ways and fall into the pattern of being the kind of wife who would let her husband be an extension of her father and the ultimate authority on everything. But I cannot do this. I am comfortable only when sharing on an equal basis as adult-to-adult. The only exception to this is when we play and let ourselves be children again. That's fun.

We came to see you once after we were married and were having problems. You told us that you felt there was a great deal of love between us, in spite of our differences and misunderstandings. I have thought a lot about that since then. I am sending you a copy of a letter that I wrote to Bill that will show that you were correct in your feelings.

The letter, a copy of which Jenny sent me, was a "Merry Christmas" greeting to "friend and husband." She began by talking about the discussions they sometimes had in which her attempts to give honest information to Bill about what was upsetting her was heard by him as criticism. She worried that with all of the negativity of these talks her positive feelings about him might become lost. In her letter she told him what she liked most about him: his ability to come to understand her and take her interests in stride, his consideration, his generosity and sharing, his lack of prejudice, his energetic enthusiasm about even the littlest of tasks, his sense of humor, his appreciation of things done for him, his punctuality and orderliness, and an unthreatened masculinity that let him hug and kiss male friends with whom he was close. She finished:

So you see, though it is hard for me to say these things with words on my lips, I do feel them and I am happy with you—and the best of all is that when I spill over with speaking out my thoughts and some of my frustrations, that it is accepted and allowed and I'm given more and more space and time in which to continue to grow in my own way under my own direction.

Jenny's note to me reflected on the uniqueness of her family tie with Bill and their shared memories. Their long relationship prior to their marriage gave them an important center which served as a nucleus for their relationship. She felt that without this added area of caring, people with such divergent views as theirs would never be able to make it together. She concluded her note with speculations about marriage for older people:

If I were to advise people over fifty about marriage (especially if the two have a big age difference between them), I would say: talk long and hard first about what you truly value. Be wary of trying to match up with someone who feels very differently about things than you do. Actually, this is true for any age, not just those of us who are older. Don't trust love to do it all.

I also think that the attitudes and understandings about children should be discussed. My children are not perfect, but they are mine. I wish to see them as tops. Anyone who loves me understands this and gives me the gift of freedom in the way I relate to my children. Bill and I have differences about my children's looks and behavior. We thought we had talked out most things in the weeks before our wedding, but I realize now that the importance of the acceptance of my offspring as they are wasn't made entirely clear to him then. It is still a vulnerable point with me.

The things that make for a good marriage, at least for us, are a sense of humor and a sense of dignity for each of the partners. Both are absolutely necessary. So is the policy of never asking the other person to change anything about himself in order to please you. It helps to have no expectations. Then everything nice that happens can be accepted as a plus, as a gift. My constant task is to find ways to enrich Bill's life without diminishing my own personhood. I guard that personhood with my life. Without that individuality, I would not care to live. Both Bill and I like to feel a certain kind of power, the power to bring joy to the other and the power of being able to know that we are important, that we truly exist as ourselves and have meaning. We want to feel "in the know" and "in control," but we have to be careful not to put the other person down in order to experience these feelings for ourselves.

The caring that slowly developed over a long period of time for Bill and me has now become a "married caring." It is what sustains us. Without it, we would not have a relationship at all.

The relationship between Jenny and Bill is an unusual one. I don't cite it as a typical example. But few marriages among older people are "typical." The individuals involved have already had long and full lives. They bring to their new relationship all of what they have become over the years. As Jenny points out, this can create major difficulties, especially if complicated by a big age difference. Values, habits, interests, and ways of living become ingrained over the years. It is hard to change them, to fit them together with those of someone else. Yet, there is just as great richness of discovery possible for older people who come together as there is for younger Romeos and Juliets. Both Bill and Jenny have a lot to give to one another, a lot to learn from one another, and a lot of mutual growth possible in their relationship. Knowing them as I do, I can assure you that the latter is happening— and *is* mutual.

SOME ADDED THOUGHTS

All of the things I have said about the choice of marriage and the issues of marriage apply as much to older couples as to younger ones. There are some additional things about marriage in the later years that ought to be added, however.

The first is that the end of marriage looms closer for older newlyweds—an end not by divorce but by death. Although all people entering marriage ought to consider developing the kinds of skills and strength necessary to live fruitfully after the death of a spouse, this is especially important for older people. One of the problems my aunt faced, after becoming a bride in her 60s and beginning a "new" life, was forgetting how she had managed to survive in a satisfying way before she was "swept off her feet." She had been an active and self-sufficient woman as a single person, but she lost much of her self-sufficiency in giving strength to her husband in exchange for his companionship and care. When he died she found herself unable to put life back together for herself. This woman, who, other than my parents, was the most significant adult in my life, lived on without being able to regain her former spirit and vitality. Her marriage, though she enjoyed it while it lasted, dampened her future, rather than freed her for it. Being involved in a non-freeing relationship, as Jenny warns, is bound to create problems of adjustment for the surviving spouse.

The second thing to be remembered is that a relationship in depth requires a lot of involvement and emotional energy. This is true even of the "companionship" marriages being talked about by older people. If two people are to be the kinds of friends required for marriage, they had better be prepared for a depth of involvement difficult for those who have been living alone. This is not a problem unique to older people, but it can be accentuated by long developed habits and routines. For this reason, older people should allow themselves time to get to know each other; this is as important for older as for younger people. There is no reason to let one's age ruin the joy of a developing relationship. Romance is delightful at any age; no one is too old to enjoy it Relationships develop at their own speed. To rush the process is to risk killing its possibilities.

The last issue I would like to raise is that of children. Jenny and Bill had differences about how her children should behave. Because her children were still in the early stages of their adult development, it was easy for them to be faulted. "If those children were mine . . ." is a phrase often used by a spouse when relating to his or her partner's children.

There is another side to this kind of parent/child relationship. Children often have problems with their parent's choice of a new spouse. Just as spouses have no choice about the families that go along with their partners, children have no choice (although there is no doubt they have a strong influence) about their new step-parents. They may not like the choice. They may not even like the idea that their parents have a choice! Older people often complain that their children become upset when the parents begin to develop romantic feelings and to act on them. This is part of the agism described by Simone de Beauvoir. While it may be difficult for older people to escape the force of this oppression, the secret to freedom from it is the same as that of freedom from any oppression. Older people must begin by exerting their own emotional rights. Children's feelings ought to be respected by parents, but not at the expense of the parents' own freedom and dignity. Caring for our children does not mean being bound to them.

Being older yet alive in marriage is not only possible; it is desirable. Our relational lives ought not to have to die until our bodies do, whether the spouse with whom we are now committed remains with us or not.

13

To the Stone Age and Back

As an anthropologist looking at cultures all the way from the Stone Age back to the present, Margaret Mead found herself concluding that there never was and probably never will be a society in which marriage is not a primary and highly valued form of relationship. My experience, both personal and professional, leads me to the same conclusion. Yet, we could be wrong. For this reason it is important to take one last look at the question of whether, in our kind of society, the option of marriage will continue to be workable. As we move into an era in what is turning out to be, contrary to Charles Reich's prediction, a rather "ungreened" America, it is important to ask if marriage will continue to be the fruitful kind of option I have claimed.

The romantic small-town models of marriage—the hand-holding courtships, brides of whose fathers permission had to be sought for marriage, family life in quiet cottages, and all the rest—are now seen to be as unrealistic and unsuited to most people as they, in fact, have always been. But proven equally unworkable, for most of us, are the other models too—those great, but confusing, experiments of the past decade or so. The attraction of most of these models was that they were "pruriently" interesting, with all that the phrase implies. I was, personally, as intrigued as anyone could be with the possibility that more sexual and intimate freedom might provide a healthier way to live than the restricted monogamous existence to which most of us had been conditioned. The trouble for most of us who tried the experi-

ments was that those options most "pruriently" appealing—
sexually open communal or single life, swinging group marriage, or relationships based on sex just for the fun of it—
proved neither to be fun nor viable lifestyles in any other
sense. This wasn't because we thought we were being immoral
or needed to return to "decent" living but because most of the
experimental lifestyles turned out to be unsatisfying. They
lost their appeal because in trying to live them out people
tended to end up feeling lonely and sad.

As I have reviewed the sorts of relationships to which
people are now turning, it is apparent that the most common
are paired ones. In the beginning of such relationships there
is the kind of process of gradual committing—the coming to
"know" one another, which I have discussed. Increasingly—
and some see this as a challenge to lasting relationships—
many couples still in the process of committing are going
ahead and living together, rather than sneaking in their
lovemaking on the side as though it weren't *really* a part of
their relationship. This makes sense, at least when the relationships are serious ones in which the individuals are ready
to share themselves fully with each other. Margaret Mead is
correct in saying that people can't "try" marriage. But they
can risk the sort of deep and knowing involvement out of
which a good marital relationship at least has a chance of
growing. *No* couple should decide to marry until they know
each other deeply enough to be sure of each other's ability to
live trustingly and happily with the commitment to care responsibly.

My wife and I went through a lot before our living together
became acceptable enough to our families and those who
knew us so that we no longer felt under pressure to change
our personal lives. We had both seen how susceptible to disas-
ter were marriages undertaken under such pressure. Acceptance finally came and, with it, both a feeling of freedom
and a desire to make formal and public our commitment to
each other. It was at this point, and only at this point, that we
could decide to celebrate our marriage and announce it to the
world.

It is when the decision to marry is a free one that it means the most. If the individuals in a couple do not *have* to choose to legalize their relationship, their decision can be made on a wholehearted belief that they wish to freely take upon them-selves the commitment required of marriage.

THE MARRIAGE OPTION

Marriage is only one of many options for an adult in today's world. Both "arrangements" and group living are possible, and for some they may be better options than a formalized centered relationship. The same is true for being a single adult—and I do not just mean not-yet-married or unlikely-to-be-married people. For many adults, remaining or becom-ing single is an attractive and viable option as a lifestyle. If a person's choice of non-attachment to another individual is a flight from relationships, it is likely to mean a lonely life. But if it is, instead, a decision to reach out in interaction to many others from a stance of secure and self-valuing singleness, then it need not be lonely at all. Singleness can be a positive and self-affirming option, with the same kind of chances for happiness and the same dangers of unhappiness as offered to those who wish to invest themselves in a special continuing and committed relationship with someone else.

The existence of all of these other options, however, does not diminish the value and worth of marriage. In fact, since one no longer *has* to be married to be accepted in society, the option of marriage becomes more meaningful than ever. One has to have good reasons to marry and good reasons to con-tinue a marriage. Because of the freedom we have had to redefine what marriage is and because of the knowing in-vestment and personal commitment required in our era of multiple options, the marriages of people today have pos-sibilities within them unknown in more traditional times.

America has not greened in the way the optimists and ex-perimenters of the late 60s hoped. This has disappointed many, but not me. I would have enjoyed the greening, perhaps. My dreams and fantasies were delightfully stimulated by the prospects. But I continue to want to live well and to be able to fulfill as much of my personal potential as I decided was important during my come-outer days of not so long ago. I have discovered, along with many other experimenters, that the committed and caring lifestyles evolving in our not-so-green America seem better able to help this happen than either those from the recent past or those romantic, but unrealistic, models from more distant times. In spite of all the problems with which we must deal in America, it feels good to be alive now and to be able to celebrate and affirm with people their choice to joyously commit themselves to ongoing and deeply knowing centered relationships.

Margaret Mead, in her usual wisdom, was right in saying that marriage has always been with us and always will be. There are good reasons for people to want to choose the marriage option. Personally, it is an option whose choice has had more meaning and importance in my life than any other decision I have ever made. It has brought a sharing of love and joy and personal growth with two fine women and five beautiful children.

"There is a time and a place for every purpose under heaven. A time to be born and a time to die . . ." and thank whatever gods may be that, in between, there is also a time for marriage. For as the poet e.e. cummings so beautifully puts it, we "can dance our deaths away" at our weddings.

Bibliography

Bach, George R., and Ronald M. Deutsch, *Pairing* (New York: Peter H. Wyden, Inc., 1970).

———, and Peter H. Wyden, *The Intimate Enemy* (New York: William Morrow & Co., Inc., 1969).

Buber, Martin, *I and Thou* (New York: Charles Scribner's Sons, 1958).

Camus, Albert, *The Fall* (New York: Alfred A. Knopf, Inc., 1957).

Cooper, David, *Death of the Family* (New York: Pantheon, 1970).

Cummings, E. E., *Complete Poems, 1913–1962* (New York: Harcourt, Brace, Jovanovich, 1972).

de Beauvoir, Simone, *The Coming of Age* (New York: G. P. Putnam's Sons, 1972).

———, *The Second Sex* (New York: Alfred A. Knopf, Inc., 1953).

Erikson, Erik H., *Childhood and Society*, 2nd ed. (W. W. Norton & Co., Inc., 1964).

Fingarette, Herbert, *The Self in Transformation* (New York: Basic Books, Inc., 1963).

Firestone, Shulamith, *The Dialectic of Sex* (New York: William Morrow & Co., 1974).

Fromm, Erich, *The Art of Loving* (New York: Harper & Row, 1956).

Gottlieb, David, ed., *Children's Liberation* (Englewood Cliffs, N. J.: Prentice-Hall, 1973).

Grollman, Earl A., *Explaining Divorce to Children* (Boston: Beacon Press, 1969).

———, *Talking About Divorce* (Boston: Beacon Press, 1975).

Haven, Susan, and David Klein, *Seven Perfect Marriages That Failed* (New York: Stein & Day, 1975).

Lederer, William J., and Don D. Jackson, *The Mirages of Marriage* (New York: W. W. Norton & Co., Inc., 1968).

Mazur, Ronald M., *Commonsense Sex* (Boston: Beacon Press, 1968).

———, *The New Intimacy* (Boston: Beacon Press, 1973).

McCafferty, Danelle, *Celebration! The Wild Flower Write Your Own Ceremony Picnic Reception Wedding Book* (New York, Pocket Books, Inc., 1974).

Mead, Margaret, *Blackberry Winter* (New York: William Morrow & Co., Inc., 1972).

O'Neill, Nena and George, *Open Marriage* (New York: M. Evans & Co., Inc., 1972).

———, *Shifting Gears* (New York: M. Evans & Co., Inc., 1974).

Otto, Herbert, *New Sexuality* (Palo Alto: Science & Behavior Books, Inc., 1971).

Powell, John, *The Secret of Staying in Love* (Niles, Ill.: Argus Communications, 1974).

Reich, Charles, *The Greening of America* (New York: Random House, Inc., 1970).

Rimmer, Robert H., *Proposition 31* (New York: The New American Library, 1971).

Rogers, Carl, *Becoming Partners* (New York: Delacorte Press, 1972).

Rubin, Theodore, *Compassion and Self-Hate* (New York: David McKay, 1975).

———, *The Angry Book* (New York: The Macmillan Co., 1969).

Russell, Bertrand, *Marriage and Morals* (New York: Liveright, 1970).

Sheehy, Gail, *Passages* (New York: E. P. Dutton & Co., Inc., 1976).

Tillich, Hannah, *From Time to Time* (New York: Stein & Day, 1973).

Whitman, Walt, *Leaves of Grass* (New York: Random House, Inc., The Modern Library, 1940).